THE
C.A.P.E.
CRUSADE

Your Guide to a Great College Application Personal Essay

Billy Lombardo

Printed in the United States of America

Paperback ISBN: 9781958714140
Ebook ISBN: 9781958714157

Library of Congress Control Number: 2022942967

CHICAGO · NEW YORK · PARIS · ROME
Muse Literary
3319 N. Cicero Avenue
Chicago IL 60641-9998

For Johnny Lombardo,

who knew how to live.

Why The C.A.P.E. Crusade Is the Book for You

The books that are already out there on the college essay are fine, and I encourage you to skim all of them before making a choice. They've been around for a long time for good reason; they're thoughtful and measured, and they're written by people who know the college admissions world.

They include sections such as "there are four types of this," "five easy steps to this," and "these are topics never to write about...."

But there aren't just four types. There aren't just five easy steps. And there aren't topics "never to write about." There are topics you should probably be very careful with, of course, but a great writer could write a great essay on any topic. And the best topic in the world can turn into a terrible essay.

I'm not from the world of college counseling, and I didn't have to write an essay to get into college. I didn't ace the ACT, I didn't even *take* the SAT, and somehow I still got into college. Somehow, I also got a master's degree. And though I grew up in a house with no books, I somehow became an award-winning writer.

By incorporating lessons I've learned through decades of immersing myself in the scholarship of literature and the craft of creative writing, I've published in every literary genre—from articles, reviews, interviews, and essays, to poetry, flash fiction, nonfiction, short stories, novels, and plays.

In the world of publishing, the author sends their work to the publisher, and they call the editor who makes the final decision on whether to accept or reject the work, the *acquisitions editor*.

In effect, you are sending your **C**ollege **A**pplication **P**ersonal **E**ssay (your **C.A.P.E.**) to a kind of acquisitions editor, the admissions officer who will determine whether or not your essay adds to, or subtracts from, your complete student application.

It's a kind of publication. So, you have to make a positive impression on your reader. In order to get "published," you have to *move* your reader. You have to have a positive impact on your reader.

It's not like writing an essay for your English teacher who will give you a good grade if you just avoid the words *truly* and *relatable* and *overall* and *basically*. It's not like writing an essay for your history teacher, who you know will give you an A if your topic sentences are tight, your introduction is captivating, and your conclusion wraps up the essay in a pretty bow tie.

You're writing your **C**ollege **A**pplication **P**ersonal **E**ssay—an essay unlike anything you've ever written—and you're writing it for a reader you don't know. The reader could be an old pro or brand new to the world of college admissions; they could be fully versed in your complete application or a hired gun whose only role is to read application essays.

This book is intended to prepare you to write a successful essay, no matter who your audience is. It builds on lessons I've learned through decades of teaching, studying the craft of writing, and coaching hundreds of students from around the world to great **C**ollege **A**pplication **P**ersonal **E**ssays.

It includes topics not addressed in other books on the college essay. Among them...

- Myths, complaints, and challenges of the College Application Personal Essay
- An inexhaustible list of essay topics other books ignore
- C.A.P.E. prompts
- Working with mentors
- Braiding together seemingly disconnected topics
- A section on memory
- The characteristics of great personal essays
- Re-thinking the first draft
- Common (and flawed) approaches to the C.A.P.E.

Whether you happened upon this book on your own or someone recommended it to you, whether someone who loves you put it in your hands or dropped it on your desk—you're about to start your C.A.P.E. Crusade.

Contents

Preface

They're making me call this a book. After all, it's got a front and back cover, a publisher, a table of contents, a preface, an introduction, acknowledgments, and all that stuff that comes with being a book. All of which makes you a *reader*.

But as much as anything, *The C.A.P.E. Crusade* is a *course*, the purpose of which is to take you through every phase of the College Application Personal Essay, from generating ideas for the topic, to writing the discovery draft, to crafting the final draft. It includes information and tips and strategies and assignments; all the stuff that comes with being a course. All of which makes you a *participant*.

You come from all walks of life. Some of you will have some kind of support through the college application process, and some of you (as was the case with me) will go through the process largely on your own. Some of you attend schools with well-staffed teams of college counselors; others come from schools whose counselors each have more than a hundred students whose college application paths they're responsible for preparing. Some of you have been thinking about college since eighth grade, and some of you have only just begun thinking about the possibility that college might be in the future.

This book is intended to help all of you with one element of the college application process: The College Application Personal Essay, a term I will use interchangeably with its acronym: the C.A.P.E.

Whether you've got a team of people ready to support you through the college application process or whether you're mostly on your own, this book is intended to help guide you from the idea generation phase straight through to the final draft of the **College Application Personal Essay.**

This is not a process you can mad-lib your way through. It's not a template or boilerplate for the perfect college essay. My intention is to equip you with the information, advice, strategies, tips, tricks, and tools to help you bring out the best **College Application Personal Essay** you have within you.

Why C.A.P.E.?

The three terms most commonly used for the essay that high school seniors write for their college application are the *Common App Essay*, the *College Essay*, and the *Personal Statement*.

None of them are perfect.

The term *Common App Essay* gets its name from The Common Application, the non-profit organization created to simplify the application process for college candidates. It started with fifteen higher learning organizations and now represents something like nine hundred.

The term *Common App Essay* describes, in two and a half words, exactly what the function of the essay is; it refers to the essay portion of the Common Application, but it provides no other information about the essay.

The worst part of the title, though, is that you want your essay to be anything but common.

The term *College Essay* is even less effective in its ability to describe the document. Do an online search for *"College Essay,"* and you'll likely be referred to more articles on college analytical essays than anything else.

As for the final term, *Personal Statement,* the word *personal* is important, as you'll soon learn, but the word *statement* doesn't quite do it for me.

"I stand for justice" is a personal statement, too, but in your application to get into the school of your dreams, "I stand for justice" probably won't tip the scales in your favor.

I like to think of this as the **C**ollege **A**pplication **P**ersonal **E**ssay, because it says it all. It's a personal essay for the college application. Also, C.A.P.E. is a pretty sweet acronym.

Let this moment begin your crusade for the best C.A.P.E. you have within you.

Introduction

You're on the verge of an important element of the college application process—the College Application Personal Essay (C.A.P.E.).

Maybe you've been looking forward to it, maybe you've been dreading it, or maybe you're thinking of it as just another hurdle you've got to get past to move on to the next phase of your life. But wherever you fall on the excitement/dread continuum, it's important to see the College Application Personal Essay for what it is.

The College Application Personal Essay is a 650-word personal statement required by an overwhelming majority of schools.

The C.A.P.E. is one of five elements of your college application profile; the other four elements are 1) your grades and coursework, 2) your extracurricular history, 3) your ACT/SAT test scores, and 4) your recommendations and interviews.

I'm not sure anyone involved in the college admissions arena would be completely comfortable assigning precise weights to each of these elements, but if I were pressed to assign a scale, it might look something like this:

- Grades and coursework (20%)
- Extracurricular history (30%)
- ACT/SAT scores (15%)
- Recommendations and interviews (10%)
- College Application Personal Essay (25%)

In the *before* times, test scores were given more weight, but for a variety of reasons, many colleges and universities have been rethinking the prominence of test scores over the last few years. Though COVID-19 seems to have thrust the test-optional movement forward, other factors have also been in play.

Admissions personnel at the various schools to which you apply might assign slightly different percentages to these pieces of your student profile. In other words, this scale is not a science. No college or university is likely to publicize the weight they might give each of these five elements in their admissions materials.

But this *is* a certainty: roughly 3/4 of your student profile is officially behind you. Any potential interviews are probably still ahead (but few people in the business will argue for the value of the interviews, anyway), and your recommendation letters might not have been written yet, but your grades, your coursework, your extracurricular history, and your test scores are largely established history.

The one element of your student profile that is still entirely under your control is your **C**ollege **A**pplication **P**ersonal **E**ssay. This piece of the puzzle is still within the boundaries of your control.

And that's what I'm here to help you with.

Team You

I'll use the term *Team You* a couple of times throughout this book, primarily at times when it will be helpful to enlist the people around you with one or more steps in the process of writing your College Application Personal Essay.

For our purposes, *Team You* includes you and anyone else that you enlist to be on your support team through the creation of your C.A.P.E. Their role may be as simple as reading the C.A.P.E. prompts to you to get you started on generating ideas or as involved as taking notes while you dictate your extended responses, interviewing you through the C.A.P.E. follow-up assignments, or being interviewed for the memory assignment. Or their role may include reading and proofreading every draft of your essay and helping you pare your C.A.P.E. down from 3000 words to 650.

Team You could include friends, teammates, siblings, parents, other relatives, coaches, counselors, therapists, teachers, neighbors, bosses, and co-workers. It certainly helps if they know you well, and it's a bonus if they happen to be good writers.

I've been a teacher for more than three decades, so I know full well that some of you will go through this experience largely on your own. My own parents played no role in my application to college. For a long time I thought I was the only person on *Team Me*, but as soon as I made an effort to reach out to others at my school, I learned that I didn't have to go through the process totally on my own.

This book was created to assist you whether you've got only one person on *Team You* (yourself) or a dozen, but it will certainly help if you've got at least one other person you can bring onto your team.

CHAPTER 1
Pre-Thinking: Defining, Questioning, Setting the Stage

Think of this section as an introduction to the College Application Personal Essay, or C.A.P.E.

Section One was designed to lay the foundation for your C.A.P.E. and to provide you with the informative context for this essential element of the college application process. I hope this section will ease you into a reflective mindset and prepare you for the thoughtful work ahead.

All You Need to Know about the C.A.P.E.

As I mentioned above, the majority of schools to which you apply will ask you to submit a **College Application Personal Essay.** The C.A.P.E. is a 650-word personal essay that all schools using the Common App will see. Every college *chooses* whether or not to require a personal essay, but even if the C.A.P.E. is not required, you still have the option to submit an essay. And it is an option well worth your consideration.

Parties on both sides of the college essay—you and the admissions officer—want your essay to portray you as a human being beyond your grades, statistics, and test scores, and perhaps even beyond your life as a student.

The C.A.P.E. is not a narrative take on your resume

Your essay should focus on elements of your life that are not reflected in the other parts of your application. If you think of this essay as just another version of your resume, you'll be missing one of your best opportunities for the admissions committee to get to know you.

Self-reflection

One of the most important elements of the personal essay is self-reflection. Your capacity as a self-reflecting human being says something about your individual journey and your capacity for growth and maturity. Nothing else in your college application will provide admissions professionals with a better sense of who you are as a self-reflecting human than your **College Application Personal Essay.**

How important is the college essay?

As was mentioned in the introduction, most college counselors agree that essays can account for about 25 percent of your admissions decision. And now, as many colleges are becoming ACT- and SAT-optional, some college counselors believe that the college essay will have even greater weight.

Why is it important?

The C.A.P.E. is a chance to speak *directly* to the admissions office. No matter what your numbers, scores, and statistics, there are plenty of college applicants out there with similar numbers, scores, and statistics.

And more importantly, whatever your scores and statistics look like—I can't emphasize this enough—you are *more* than those numbers, and you want the admissions teams to know this.

One way to think about it is that when college admissions teams see your file, absent the college essay, they only see you as two-dimensional—they see the length and the breadth of your academic, athletic, and extracurricular achievements, but it isn't so easy for them to see beyond those surface elements of your profile. The essay is an opportunity for them to get at your depth, your substance, and your personality—the story beneath.

Tell me something I don't know

"Tell me something I don't know" was one of the most annoying things kids said to each other back when I was a kid—maybe they still say it—but it's helpful, here, to think of admissions officers as

21

having this statement in a thought balloon over their heads while reading your essay. You want your C.A.P.E. to tell college admissions officers something they don't already know about you.

If you're an Olympic-level equestrian, your profile already shows it. If you've dedicated yourself to the service of others, your profile shows it. If you nailed the SAT and the ACT and have never received anything less than an A+, your profile shows it.

Imagine the admissions officer reading the essay of a Division I–ready athlete who writes an essay that doesn't even hint at their athletic history. That is much more likely to make an impact on the admissions officer than an essay that addresses the essayist's athletic history.

This doesn't mean there can't be some overlap with another element of your profile. But if your essay addresses *anything* that's already included in your application, it should expand deeply and meaningfully on that subject.

Where to begin?

In an upcoming section, I'll share the 2022–2023 Common App essay prompts, which you may already be aware of. They're intended to be broad and open-ended, but I have found that using the Common App prompts as a starting point sometimes does more to limit the breadth and depth of essay topics than expand them.

I promise you that this course will help you prepare an essay that will be a direct response to at least one of the essay prompts, even if you don't set your eyes on them until after your final draft is ready to go.

What do I write about?

What you *choose* to write about shows admissions teams what you see as important, and *how* you write about it offers them a great opportunity to learn things about you that they're not going to find anywhere else in your profile.

These prompts and my years of experience in guiding students through this process will help you choose from the countless possibilities of subjects you have to write about.

Myths, Complaints, and a Few *Actual* Challenges of the College App Personal Essay

Not every college applicant is inclined to do a happy dance when it comes to thinking about the **College Application Personal Essay.** The good news is this: the myths and complaints—though numerous and common—are, in the end, just that: myths and complaints. And the actual challenges are, as you'll find out soon, conquerable hurdles. And the goal of this book is to help you conquer them.

Because they're so widely held and so usually false, let's get the myths out of the way.

MYTHS ABOUT THE C.A.P.E.

Myth #1: I won't get into college without a brilliant, mind-blowing essay.

First of all, as I addressed in the introduction, the **College Application Personal Essay** is only one of the five elements of the college application; the others are GPA, test scores, recommendations & interviews, and extracurriculars. And just as there are plenty of students in colleges with GPAs, test scores, recommendations, and extracurricular histories that are less than stellar, colleges and universities are filled with students whose **College Application Personal Essays** have fallen short of blowing any minds.

As I'll discuss in greater detail in a few pages, the purpose of the C.A.P.E. is for your colleges to know who you are, if you're ready to write at the college level, and if you've got a pretty good shot at thriving on their campus. You can do all of these things without writing a miraculous essay.

Myth #2: I've heard that the best college essays are written by students who have experienced dramatic events. I can't compete with that.

The best college essays are great, not because they describe an exciting or dramatic event, but because they convey an interesting way of looking at the world. In 2016, Brittany Stinson's college essay about shopping at Costco went viral after she was accepted into five Ivy League schools. I don't know much more about Stinson's life, but unless she lived her life in a bubble, I'm guessing she had at least some drama greater than a Costco visit. The point is, you don't have to wow your readers with some dramatic experience. Your goal should be to write about something that is meaningful to you and to convey that meaning in your writing.

Myth #3: Everyone I know has a more amazing story than I do.

The accomplishments, successes, gifts, talents, and skill sets of other people have nothing to do with you. Admissions teams want to know how you see the world, how you live in the world, and how you move through the world. The idea isn't to write an epic story. Your essay should say something about how you think, what you stand for, who you are, and what you want to be. You're a work in progress, and they know that. If you were already at the peak of your knowledge, the top of your game, the best you could be at everything, maybe you should think about starting your own university instead of merely attending one.

Myth #4: So many college essays are about overcoming adversity. I've had a pretty challenge-free existence (until this college application process came along).

There is no doubt that overcoming challenges is a common essay topic; the second Common App essay prompt actually addresses this topic directly.

Like most of us, college admissions officers are well aware that some people have had significant challenges to overcome in their lives. But they are not in the business of comparing one student's experience with another to find out who has suffered the most.

And as we've hinted at with Brittany Stinson's Costco essay, there are many C.A.P.E.s that have little or nothing to do with overcoming adversity.

Myth #5: The college essay is supposed to be intensely personal.

The point of the C.A.P.E. is not to delve into your deepest and darkest secrets; it's to show colleges who you are and how you might thrive, and contribute to, the college campus. The C.A.P.E. is not the appropriate arena for your deepest and darkest secrets. There are absolutely some topics that are inappropriate material for this essay. Experiences related to drugs and crime and sex, calling in-depth attention to personality flaws, and calling attention to unresolved mental health issues are just a few examples that are probably inappropriate topics for the college essay. I urge you toward meaningful and deliberate self-reflection but revealing something very private may be interpreted as inappropriate. This is not the space for raising red flags.

Myth #6: I've actually had pretty significant challenges that I've overcome, but I don't want to write about them.

This is probably one of the most commonly accepted myths about the College Application Personal Essay. You'll hear it from teachers and guidance counselors to friends, neighbors, and relatives. More than once, I have actually heard veteran teachers say, in response to actual tragedies that befall students, that a good essay can come of the event.

Every student has more than one personal essay in them. We are, all of us, layered and complex individuals whose lives cannot always be summed up in a single 650-word essay. How we face challenges does say something about us, but each of us is more than the challenges we face.

I have worked with students who have written great essays that have nothing to do with adversity, and I've worked with students who have had major challenges that aren't even mentioned in their essays.

It's not an uncommon topic, so it's not impossible to imagine that a stack of essays might contain several Overcoming Adversity themes. So, imagine that the admissions officer reading your essay has just read five applications of students whose essays are about overcoming adversity. If I were you, some part of me would be wondering how my pain compares to the pain of the other applicants.

That's not the best mindset for creative writing. You don't want to be comparing your anguish to the anguish of others when you're sitting down to write your essay, but you should understand that there *are* people who do this. We all hope that our essay will be read by a

27

measured and responsible, thoughtful and understanding, seasoned college admissions officer, but that might not be the case.

It bears repeating. You are more than the challenges you have faced.

The focus of your essay has to be about who you are as a person and not "are my challenges enough."

In May of 2021, Elijah Megginson, a graduating senior at Uncommon Charter High School in Crown Heights, Brooklyn, wrote an opinion piece in the *New York Times* titled, "When I Applied to College, I Didn't Want to Sell My Pain."

The article addresses the issue rather nicely and is worth the trouble of a search.

COMPLAINTS ABOUT THE C.A.P.E.

...In which I call attention to mostly unfounded complaints about the College Application Personal Essay.

Complaint #1: After four years of playing the game, this is just one more ridiculous hoop to jump through.

For some students, the exercise of writing a personal essay for college feels disingenuous and performative—just another hoop they have to jump through to get into college.

It feels icky. I get it. But there's actually great value in reflecting on the story of your life and in taking the time to write it clearly and precisely. The C.A.P.E. can have value far beyond its value to the college admissions process.

One of the questions I ask students who I have coached through the C.A.P.E. process is: *What surprised you about your responses to the C.A.P.E. idea generation prompts?*

Frequently, college applicants tell us that they were surprised they responded to the prompts so personally, thoughtfully, and thoroughly.

It's not because the C.A.P.E. prompts are astoundingly brilliant and provocative. It's much more likely that early on in the process of writing their C.A.P.E., students quickly begin to understand the immense value of self-reflection on the occasions of their lives. This, in itself, raises the purpose of the C.A.P.E. beyond hoop-jumping.

Complaint #2: I'm not comfortable bragging about myself. The college essay is all about bragging.

If college admissions officers expect applicants to distinguish themselves from everyone else in the applicant pool, it's understandable that students think they're expected to use the C.A.P.E. as an opportunity to brag, and we've all been warned about the dangers of bragging.

By now, you probably understand—at least implicitly—that you can write your college essay without addressing every tremendous accomplishment of your life; you can write a great essay about nap time in kindergarten, about being a mediocre fly fisherman, a frequent shopper at Costco, or an amateur gardener.

But you probably also know that you can address your experience as an accomplished musician, athlete, actor, or juggler without being excessively proud and boastful. That kind of bragging almost always backfires.

If you guide yourself with traits such as humility, humor, and honesty, you can avoid the pitfalls of bragging while using the C.A.P.E. as an opportunity to celebrate your accomplishments.

Complaint #3: All of my friends already seem to know what they want to do with their lives. I still have no idea.

It's true that admissions folks will read plenty of essays by students who feel they already know what they want to do—and there's nothing wrong with that. It's also true that many of these seemingly focused students will change their minds along the way.

More importantly, though, every admissions officer understands it's okay not to have a clear vision of the future. College is a place and time for you to explore and unfold and decide what path you want to pursue.

And there's something refreshing about reading the essays of students who are clearly aware that their university years are meant to be about learning, exploring, taking detours, and making discoveries.

CHALLENGES OF THE C.A.P.E.

For many students, there are actual challenges to overcome when it comes to the College Application Personal Essay. In this section, I address these challenges with the hope of helping reluctant essayists get past them.

Challenge #1: The college essay calls for a different kind of writing than I'm used to.

This is true for almost everyone. The only students for whom it's not true are the students who are lucky enough to have been introduced to the personal essay form.

For everyone else, it's a completely different kind of writing than what high school students are used to. After four years of being told to write from the third-person point of view and to *keep the "I" out of your analytical essays,* you're being asked to write a personal essay from the first-person point of view.

Challenge #2: I've got to get my entire personality in a 650-word essay.

Half true. You do have only 650 words, which is probably not enough real estate in which to stuff the massive gorgeousness of your personality, but you don't have to get your *entire* personality in the essay.

A few things to ease your mind:

1. Think of the essay as an opportunity to just get *some* of your personality into the essay.
2. Don't focus on the limitations of the word count; if you head into the essay too focused on word count, you'll never get to the discoveries necessary for a great essay.
3. You may have to reach out to an experienced writer, teacher, relative, friend, etcetera, who has an editor's mind and heart, but anyone who knows what they're doing with an editor's pencil will be able to take your 3000-word discovery draft down to 650 words.

31

Challenge #3: Writing isn't easy.

This is true. I'm sorry. Every writing project comes with its own set of problems, and our responsibility is to find solutions to the particular problems of the College Application Personal Essay.

I am definitely not saying that the college essay is a walk in the park—like every writing assignment, the college essay is an exercise in problem-solving. This book is here to help you solve the problems of the C.A.P.E.

The Three-Pronged Purpose of the C.A.P.E.

In a nutshell, college admissions officers are looking to learn three things about you in your essay:

1. Who are you?
2. Will you thrive on *our** campus?
   a. Will you benefit from life on *our** campus?
   b. Will you contribute to life on *our** campus?
3. Is your writing college-ready?

We'll take some time in this section to address each of these responsibilities of the C.A.P.E.

* I'll explain why I italicize this word in the section on thriving below.

Who Are You?

Admissions officers are responsible for selecting the students who will live in their dorms and apartments, engage in their courses, eat in their cafeterias, play in their fields and gyms, participate in their clubs, relax in their courtyards, and study in their libraries and laboratories. They want to know what kind of person you are and how you move through the world. They want to know if their college is right for you and if you'll be a good fit for them.

All of the elements of a student's profile can help offer admissions officers a sense of who you are, but your C.A.P.E. contains a unique and spectacular opportunity to present yourself in ways that your grades, extracurriculars, and your scores do not.

Will You Thrive on *Our** Campus?

*I italicize this word to emphasize this important point: college admissions officers aren't in the business of trying to determine if you're going to thrive on *any* campus. They know, as your guidance counselors know, that there are dozens—maybe hundreds of colleges and universities that would be great, even perfect fits for you. College admissions officers are merely trying to determine (as well as they can) if you're going to thrive on *their* campus.

I think we can agree that thriving on campus can mean many things, but the bottom line is that colleges want to know if you'll both benefit from and contribute to life on their campus.

Traits of Students Who Thrive on College Campuses

We can also probably agree on at least some of the character traits that indicate a high likelihood of success in a new environment—traits such as self-awareness, introspection, resourcefulness, responsibility, maturity, and resilience. Admissions officers are interested in students who will add to the life of their campus—students who will be active and engaged members of the community.

Fortunately, there's plenty of room on every campus for a great range of other character traits as well. Traits such as optimism, hope, a sense of humor, open-mindedness, affability, intellectual curiosity, self-awareness, inclusiveness, and an appreciation for a great diversity of people and personality types. And just as there is room for a wide range of personality traits on every campus, there is room in every essay to showcase your personality.

The **C**ollege **A**pplication **P**ersonal **E**ssay is your best chance to put your personality on display—to share personal aspects of yourself that will allow admissions teams to see who you are beyond your numbers (grades, test scores, and statistics) and beyond the history revealed through the other elements of your college application.

Are You Ready for College Writing?

And finally, admissions officers want to know if your writing is college-ready. Your ability to write will play a role in the likelihood of your potential to thrive in college; much can be learned about you from your ability to write effectively, efficiently, precisely, and creatively.

The college essay is an opportunity to showcase your writing skills, your voice, and your personality. Nowhere else in your profile will these things be spotlighted. This is not meant to add to any stress you might have about the next few months. I believe, in fact, that this book, and the process of writing your C.A.P.E., will not only help you summon the best essay you have within but will help you develop your skills as a writer as well.

The C.A.P.E. Notebook

One of the discoveries I've made over years of this work is that for many writers (and regardless of what you think of *writer* as a label for yourself, it's important to think of yourself that way through the duration of this endeavor), something happens when you put pen or pencil to paper that doesn't happen when you put your fingers to the keyboard.

I encourage you to get yourself a great pencil—my favorite is the *Palomino Blackwing 602**—and a notebook—my favorite is the *National 43-581** (you can Google it to find where to purchase). It's got green lines, is easy on the eyes, is pretty inexpensive, and has a nice sturdy cover.

These two things may sound gimmicky, but they help me to think seriously about everything I put to paper.

We'll refer to the C.A.P.E. notebook often enough, but don't sweat it if keeping notes in the digital world is more your style.

* I promise I'm not sponsored by these products (but I should be).

Characteristics of the Personal Essay

Because the best college essays are personal essays, it makes a great deal of sense to look at the characteristics of the personal essay.

I have adapted these characteristics from Phillip Lopate's introduction to his book *The Art of the Personal Essay.*

The personal essay has an *apparent* subject and a *deeper* subject

This is true of poetry, short stories, novellas, novels, and College Application Personal Essays. In all good works of art there are at least two stories. Very often one is on the surface, and one is submerged. Jane Hirschfield says, "Every good poem wrestles with something that matters."

Very often, in all literary genres, the wrestling takes place in the story *beneath.*

And at the heart of every good C.A.P.E. is something that matters, too. But it's usually not buried too far beneath the surface in the C.A.P.E.

The essays included in the addendum to this book, written by Cole and Lucy, are good examples of how this two-story method plays out in the C.A.P.E. Very often, the apparent subject is introduced at the beginning of the essay, and the deeper subject is introduced shortly after.

In the opening of Cole's Tapping In essay, the writer is playing guitar in a band with his father, and he taps his father on the shoulder to signal his desire to take over the big solo. Shortly afterward, the author moves into the deeper subject, which is about "tapping in" to life in so many other ways.

In the apparent story of Lucy's essay, the author explains that a *stay upper* is a six-year-old who has moved on from the four- and five-year-old students in her Montessori school. And as early as the second paragraph, Lucy moves into the deeper subject, which has to do with extending that *stay-upper* spirit through middle school and into high school.

The personal essay is intimate

Though the college essay is likely to include a story, it is certainly not like the *once upon a time* stories of your childhood. It's personal. No one but you could tell this story.

The effect of the personal essay is artful, literary, well-crafted

Like personal essays, the college essay is included in the genre of creative nonfiction, which is to say the college essay is nonfiction (it's true), and it's creative.

The voice and tone of the personal essay are conversational

Phillip Lopate says that "personal essayists converse with the reader because they are already having dialogues with themselves." The C.A.P.E. may have elements of the formal, but generally speaking, the tone of the personal statement is meant to be informal, casual, conversational, and personal.

The personal essay is not afraid to be emotional

Though there is no requirement that the personal statement is emotional, we are first and foremost emotional beings; our everyday habits are influenced by our emotions. Author Amy Bloom says, "You should write about things that matter to you." When you write about things that matter, you often head in the direction of emotion.

You may be inclined to think that the college essay should veer from sentiment because *sentiment is cheesy*, but it's my belief that there's a little bit of cheesiness in all powerful writing. Readers want to be moved, and in the admissions officer's eyes, there's nothing emotional about your grades, your GPA, your class rank, or your statistics on the field or court—but your essay can go there.

The personal essay shares a range of emotions

But even though the personal essay isn't afraid to be emotional, it calls for moderation, and it calls for a range of emotions. The point isn't to make the admissions officer cry from start to finish or laugh until their temples are about to explode. Happiness, sadness, fear, disgust, anger—the best essays we've read touch on more than one emotion. Like great poems, stories, and movies, great essays often include a *turn* or a *shift*—a change in thought, tone, or emotion. Think of some of the best uses of humor in writing; they work because the humor is stacked against something tender or profound—some tone other than humor.

The personal essay yearns to reveal the truth

One of my favorite aspects of any personal essay—especially the College App Personal Essay—is that it seeks to reveal the truth. In fact, it very often reveals truths to the essayist that they are not fully aware of when they sit down to write the essay. And colleges and universities very much *want* this essay to reveal the truth.

Among the most important things college counselors want their students to understand is that 1) not every college is the right fit—even if the student has had their heart set on that particular college since eighth grade; and 2) that there are great—perhaps even *perfect* colleges for every high school graduate.

The personal essay examines limitations and inconsistency

Limitations and inconsistency are two more truths that the college essay should not be afraid to reveal. Phillip Lopate says essayists are "intrigued by their limitations." They admit things that you're not always supposed to tell strangers—like punching a younger sister in the stomach (Eula Biss) and eating napkins (Chuck Klosterman). It is not an uncommon path in great literature to explore the inconsistency and wreck of humanity.

The narrator of the personal essay is reliable

Your reliability as an essayist says something about your reliability as a student.

The personal essay explores what it doesn't know

Though college essayists often take this as an opportunity to tell colleges what the applicant knows, the often-overlooked essay explores a problem that the student doesn't know how to solve. The best essays are about discovery. Writing is often an attempt to figure out what we know.

The personal essay is not afraid to examine the small things in life

Phillip Lopate says the personal essay is writing that "takes a seemingly trivial or everyday subject and then brings interest to it." Sometimes, it is your reflection on the small, perhaps unexpected subjects, that distinguish you from the rest of the applicant pool. The writer Brian Doyle begins his beautiful essay *Joyas Voladoras* by writing about a hummingbird's heart, an organ about the size of a pencil eraser. But the essay is about much more than a hummingbird's heart, a certainty that is contained in the shortest sentence in the essay: "We all churn inside."

The personal essay is not afraid of humor

This is not a comedic writing project, and comedy isn't easy to sustain in an essay, anyway, but don't be afraid to allow the reader to get a glimpse of your sense of humor in your college app personal essay.

The personal essayist isn't out to be loved by the reader

This may be a result of the essay, but it's not the goal. Lopate says, "The personal essayist is not necessarily out to win the audience's unqualified love but to present the complex portrait of a human being."

The personal essay thinks against itself, challenges its own conventional thought

If the essay is an exploration, an examination, a reflection, a search for truth, then it's very likely not a certainty. It's okay for it to question, to argue with itself. Let it be a *perhaps*.

The personal essay is flexible in form and style; it's digressive, associative.

Though stories may follow a fairly recognizable arc, the essay isn't expected to. Though it needs to come together by the end, the reader will be okay with some meandering on its way. The same thing may be said of the next characteristic of the personal essay.

The personal essay tells a good story

Like all good stories, though, we expect it to lead to a grander idea, a loftier purpose, something perhaps even beautiful.

The personal essay is uniquely singular *and* universal

Though the best college essays are profoundly individual and unique, a worthy essay ought to give the reader what Phillip Lopate spoke of as "that shiver of self-recognition ... which all readers of the personal essay await as a reward."

It's important to understand that your C.A.P.E. doesn't have to contain *all* of these personal essay characteristics, but one of the best ways for you to get, and retain, the attention and interest of the college admissions officials who read your C.A.P.E. is by paying close attention to these characteristics of the personal essay.

Essay Topics (An Inexhaustible List)

Here's a list of some essay topics we've coached students through. As you take the first steps toward writing your C.A.P.E., it might be helpful to take note of the ones that strike a chord.

- Coming to Terms with a Philosophical Quandary Essay
- This / These Photographs Say Everything Essay
- Sibling / Parent with a Great Challenge Essay
- Standing-Up-in-the-Face-of-Conflict Essay
- My Discovery / Journey / Evolution Essay
- Wilderness Camp, Outward Bound Essay
- Setback / Challenge / Obstacle Essay
- It Hasn't Been Easy to Be Me Essay
- Avocation / Hobby / Passion Essay
- Oh, the Things I've Learned Essay
- Letter to My Younger Self Essay
- Hard Work and Dedication Essay
- Mistake / Regret / Failure Essay
- My Amazing Experience Essay
- Where I'm From / Place Essay
- Special Skill / Expertise Essay
- I Can Be Annoying Essay
- Sexual Orientation Essay
- My Life Montage Essay
- Boarding School Essay
- My Year Abroad Essay
- Things I Hate Essay
- Homeschool Essay
- Eye-Opener Essay
- Role Model Essay
- Leadership Essay
- Gratitude Essay
- Culture Essay

- Family Essay
- Career Essay
- List Essay

The Common App Prompts

Though many schools also have shorter supplemental essays, one of the great things about the Common Application is that you'll write just one Common App essay for all the schools to which you are applying.

In reality, you can write about any topic you think will best tell your story, but to help you get started, the Common App provides a series of prompts. They mostly stay the same from year to year, but one of them (#4) was new in 2021–2022.

Though any one of these prompts may turn out to be a helpful starting point for essayists, over the years I've spent coaching students through the **College Application Personal Essay**, I've learned that using only one of these prompts as a guiding principle can lead to limiting the scope of your essay.

My approach to coaching you through this process is to provide you with ideas that will lead to rich essays that will likely respond more effectively, efficiently, and beautifully to more than one of the Common App prompts.

2022–23 COMMON APP ESSAY PROMPTS

1. Some students have a background, identity, interest, or talent that is so meaningful they believe their application would be incomplete without it. If this sounds like you, then please share your story.
2. The lessons we take from obstacles we encounter can be fundamental to later success. Recount a time when you faced a

challenge, setback, or failure. How did it affect you, and what did you learn from the experience?

3. Reflect on a time when you questioned or challenged a belief or idea. What prompted your thinking? What was the outcome?

4. Reflect on something that someone has done for you that has made you happy or thankful in a surprising way. How has this gratitude affected or motivated you?

5. Discuss an accomplishment, event, or realization that sparked a period of personal growth and a new understanding of yourself or others.

6. Describe a topic, idea, or concept you find so engaging that it makes you lose all track of time. Why does it captivate you? What or who do you turn to when you want to learn more?

7. Share an essay on any topic of your choice. It can be one you've already written, one that responds to a different prompt, or one of your own design.

CHAPTER 2
Pre-Writing: Recalling, Exploring, Identifying

If Chapter 1 was intended to prepare you for thinking about your
C.A.P.E., think of Chapter 2 as dedicated to the work of pre-writing.
This section was designed to help you recall and explore the stories
that have shaped you into the person you are and to identify the
threads that may connect them.

Preparing for the C.A.P.E. Crusade Prompts

PRE-PROMPT PREPARATION

I created this assignment for a couple of important reasons:

1. To get you thinking immediately about the integral stories of your life.
2. Some students begin the **College Application Personal Essay** process already having put some thought into what their C.A.P.E. topic is going to be. And though the C.A.P.E. prompts don't *always* lead essayists into completely new directions, they sometimes do. And this assignment is meant to ensure that no stone is left unturned in our attempt to get at the stories that best get at *you*.
3. Even if this book/course steers you in a completely different essay direction than the one you might be considering now, this assignment will at least give you and Team You something to think about when it comes to shaping your stories into an essay.

IF I HAD TO TURN IN MY C.A.P.E. TODAY ASSIGNMENT

If, for some horrible reason, the college application pressure was amped up in some staggering and terrible way, and you had to turn in your C.A.P.E. an hour from this very moment, what would your essay be about?

1. Generally speaking, if you had to write your **College Application Personal Essay** today, what theme (or themes) would your C.A.P.E. touch on? (Examples: my growth, my resilience, my intellectual curiosity, my deep interest in_____, etc.)
2. If you had to write your **College Application Personal Essay** today, what stories of your life (events, occasions, experiences) would you use to help illustrate the themes above?
3. Provide a paragraph or two connecting the stories in #2 (above) with the themes in #1 (above).

THE CRY OF THE OCCASION: AN INTRODUCTION TO THE C.A.P.E. STARTER PROMPTS

There's a great scene in J.D. Salinger's novella *Franny and Zooey* in which Franny says, "If you're a poet, you do something beautiful." And the poet Wallace Stevens called the poem "the cry of the occasion." Poets take the occasions of their lives and turn them into *cries* or *songs*—things of beauty.

Some of the best essays I've ever read are attempts to language the *occasions* of the student's life in the same way.

Guiding yourself through the C.A.P.E. prompts is a great way to get you started on generating ideas for your college essay. They all have to do with the *occasions* of your life. The prompts are meant to help you probe and mine and explore your occasions for what we can think of as their *literary value*.

These moments, occasions, and stories may have been emotionally charged, or challenging, beautiful, breathtaking, exhilarating, or heartbreaking—moments in which you have been made to wrestle with something important.

Your responses do not have to be in complete sentences but keep in mind that your final essay will absolutely be shaped and informed by what you produce here. The more reflective and thorough you are as you move through these prompts, the more you'll benefit from this idea generation exercise.

Some of these prompts may seem to steer you toward what may initially feel like a negative direction, but keep in mind that mistakes, failures, and regrets often lead to great essays.

Also, this is not the session to fly through in a cursory, fleeting, or skimpy manner. I'm not inclined to prioritize one session over another, but many course participants have said that this is arguably the most important session of the course. It lays the groundwork for all the sessions that follow.

This is the time to dig deep.

LAST-MINUTE ADVICE FOR C.A.P.E. PROMPTS

You are about to be guided through the C.A.P.E. prompts.

1. Don't think of this, or any section, as something you have to *get through*. It's hard to tell which section will be the one that blows open the doors to the discovery.

2. When I run my face-to-face clients through this exercise, the prompts appear on the screen for a full minute. I recommend you give yourself at least that same minute to respond.

3. For some questions, this may seem like an awfully long minute. Take that time, though, to consider the prompt carefully and thoughtfully. Get into the habit of self-reflection; the entire essay preparation process should be driven by self-reflection. Swim in the prompts that urge reflection. If your mind gets pulled in another direction, let it go there.

4. For other prompts, sixty seconds will not seem long enough. You've got two options in this case. You can disregard the time and keep writing (no one is going to honk the air horn if you let the clock ride for a couple of minutes), or you can move on to the next prompt and return to the prompts you'd like to return to later.

5. None of these prompts are meant to be rigidly adhered to. They're intended to urge forth responses that may play an important role in the development of your personal essay. If a question about a road trip makes you think of a time your car stalled on Lake Shore Drive, the prompt did its job. Tell the stalled car anecdote. If the prompt asks you to recall a story at recess and you think of Ms. Cwik, your second-grade teacher who adored you, tell the story of that angel.

6. If nothing occurs to you in that sixty seconds, it may mean you need more time to think of it; it may mean there's nothing in that prompt that will help you even if you had sixty hours for it. Move on when you feel like it. The beauty of this book is that you get to go through it on your own terms.

7. If a prompt asks you to recall a number of things (e.g., three memories, five current events) and you can only recall two,

that's fine; respond as completely as you can. And if you think of five memories or seven current events, write them all down.

8. Some of the prompts may sound similar, but these are meant to get at nuances in your response; challenge yourself to *respond beyond*.

9. It may be difficult to understand how a particular prompt could ever be capable of playing a part in a personal college essay, but each of these prompts has done just that at one time or another.

10. If a prompt seems close-ended—i.e., a prompt for which a one-word response will suffice—think of the question as having a follow-up question, such as "explain," "tell me more," and "why is that so?"

11. As suggested in Chapter 1, it's not the intention of these prompts to get you to delve into the deepest and darkest recesses of the heart and mind. You are exploring subjects for a personal college essay, and these prompts are intended only to challenge you to explore subjects you may not have considered on your own, but the terms according to which you write the essay *must* be your own terms. Though this essay is meant to be *personal*, we all have occasions and thoughts that are too heavy for the C.A.P.E.

12. This list of prompts is an ever-growing, ever-edited list; if, in responding to them, another interesting prompt occurs to you, feel free to write down the prompt *and* your response to it.

13. There are currently fifty-eight prompts here, and if you have pages and pages to write about every prompt, it will take some time to get through them. A suggestion: if you *own* a story— that is to say, that you know it so well you'll be able to come back to it easily—such as the time your kindergarten classmates

put you on trial to determine if you were a true friend—you might consider a headline as a placeholder instead of writing the whole story out—something like "Kindergarten trial, 2007." You'll get to it later if it seems as though it may turn out to inspire something.

The C.A.P.E. Prompts

1. Describe an event that took place during recess, lunchtime, a free period, in a playground, before school or after school, etc.
2. Describe an event or experience that seemed terrible when it happened but turned out to be not so bad, perhaps even positive.
3. Describe a memorable family trip.
4. Describe a negative educational experience.
5. What is your favorite room (in your home or elsewhere)? And why is it your favorite room?
6. Describe a relative who has had a major impact on you and explain why.
7. What are your three earliest memories?
8. Describe a favorite/memorable photograph. Why is it special? What makes it memorable?
9. What are pet peeves of yours?
10. Describe a time you felt you would not overcome a challenge.
11. Describe a time you were misunderstood.
12. Describe a realization you came to, a discovery you made, something you feel you figured out or solved.
13. Write about a time you acted in a way that surprised you.
14. Write about a personal failure, mistake, or regret.
15. Describe a time you said something that you wish you would not have said.
16. Write about a teacher who has had a positive impact on you.
17. If you did not have this formative experience, you might be a totally different person.
18. Name five current events that have had an effect on, or are of interest, to you.
19. Describe a family event that has impacted you.

20. Describe a time you didn't say something but wish you had.
21. Describe a positive educational experience.
22. Do you have any quirks? What are they?
23. What is one thing (or more) that drives you and motivates you to action? Pushes you to do what you do?
24. What is something people might be surprised to learn you're good at?
25. What is a character trait you dislike in people?
26. Describe a time you were offended.
27. What is a subject or activity you can get so lost in that hours can pass without notice?
28. Describe a time you misjudged someone.
29. Describe a time you realized adults don't always know what they're doing.
30. What are three events in history you are interested in?
31. What community (or communities) are important to you? And why?
32. What comes easily to you?
33. What is a time you felt angry or filled with rage?
34. If people don't know this about you, they don't know you.
35. Describe a time you felt very different from others.
36. Describe a memorable road trip.
37. What do you believe sets you apart from the crowd?
38. What is a time you felt most proud?
39. What is a worry (or worries) you have about your personal future?
40. What are the worries you have about the future of the world?
41. Who is a celebrity you would like to meet? Why?
42. What is a personal, irrational, or inexplicable fear of yours?
43. What was a time you were disappointed with someone?
44. What have you had to work hard at?

45. What is a time you were disappointed with people/the world?
46. What are some behaviors of people that drive you crazy?
47. What is a place you've never been but would like to go?
48. Tell us something that happened on a bus, train, or plane.
49. You've been invited to take part in an amazing experiment for a year. The directors of the experiment need you to just be you. You can only bring ten items with you—the essentials needed for a safe and satisfying experience will be taken care of by the directors. These items may be tangible items (your journal, a pocketknife from your grandmother; or intangible (your sense of humor, your innate curiosity). What are your ten items?
50. When was a time you were filled with hope and/or hope for the world?
51. What is a favorite place for you to go/visit?
52. Create a list of things you have, tangible or otherwise, that speak to who you are.
53. What are your plans for the coming summer?
54. You meet someone at a party who you feel immediately friendly with, and they ask you: "Tell me who you are by telling me three stories about you." What would those three stories be?
55. What is the title of a book(s) you remember someone reading to you or from your earliest days as a reader?
56. Name three books that have had an impact on you.
57. Who is a celebrity you don't care to ever meet? Why?
58. Describe a time you felt fiercely independent.

After the C.A.P.E. Prompts: Rallying the Troops of *Team You*

When I work one-on-one with college applicants, we probably connect by way of email a dozen or so times, and I might meet with them via zoom or in-person two to three times through the C.A.P.E. process.

Invariably, it is at this point in the C.A.P.E. process—right after they respond to the C.A.P.E. Prompts—that we meet face to face, if they're local, or via Zoom if they're not. I will have looked over their responses to the C.A.P.E. prompts, found some connections, highlighted some responses I'd like to hear more about, and written down a few questions for them.

I can't tell you how important it is at this point to pull someone off the bench of *Team You* and invite them into the game to take on the following roles: Interviewer and Scribe.

Team You, Position #1: The Interviewer

The role of the Interviewer can be tremendously helpful at this point.

Let me give you a recent example of the value of the Interviewer from a recent meeting with Owen, a student from the class of 2023.

Owen's original response to Prompt #1, "Describe an event that took place during recess, lunchtime, a free period, or in a playground, etc." was:

> *Freshman year I learned how to play poker and made great friends through that; they later got me into track and field.*

When I met with Owen, I asked him to tell me a little more about that experience. Here's what he said:

There's a group of people I started playing a variety of games with. It's Friday game club. It started with poker. Mahjong mostly. We played games and made core friends. It was a rotating group of people, and it became a way for me to practice social skills.

It was just good practice. I got better at things. I could devour everything about it if I got attached to it. I got myself attached to social skills and tied it up with games. And I figured out how to talk to people.

Anyway, we were playing Mahjong one day. And some of the things have numbers in Chinese, stylized calligraphy categories. You want sets. You have to know the numbers. I was playing with a lot of fluent Chinese speakers who knew all the characters. And I had to ask them what the characters meant. A year ago there was no way in the world I would have been able to ask them that simple question. And I had to ask them. I had to ask, "What does this mean?"

It was small in the grand scheme of things, but I walked away from that social situation feeling amazing, and that was a huge deal.

Because I was there to ask Owen some follow-up questions, I was able to dig a little deeper into Owen's responses. I understood his social anxiety more completely, and he was able to explain his development from a socially anxious person with a very limited friend group to a person whose interests helped him to interact with others and pushed him to take on experiences he would otherwise never have taken on.

In another of Owen's responses to a prompt about his pet peeves, Owen responded, "People who change their minds."

I might not have asked him anything about this, but elsewhere in his responses, he spoke about his love for politics and for his AP Government class, in which spirited political conversations and spirited debates took place.

So, in my follow-up interview with him, I mentioned that his pet peeve seemed a bit at odds with his interest in debate and politics. Aren't politicians always changing their minds? And isn't one of the goals of debate to change minds?

Here's how Owen responded:

Why? Why? Why? I guess it's about pushing the buttons. I find it important. That's about politics. Debating. It's acceptable to keep poking at people's arguments.

Changing a mind is hard, and it gets harder as you get older. I changed my mind when I was young, and I feel like it [saved me from a lot of trouble]; it taught me how to change my mind.

I think the same thing that makes me want to debate with people is the same thing that makes me want to change my mind. Because I want to be right. Politics made me okay with changing my mind.

The follow-up question allowed Owen not only to reconcile what seemed like contrasting ideas but also to arrive at a pretty solid articulation of his thoughts on his growth as a thinking human being.

Team You, Position #2: The Scribe

But my value on *Team Owen* for this meeting was more than just my service as an interviewer. Because I was taking notes while Owen responded to my questions, he was able to just talk freely. In effect, Owen took on the role of the storyteller.

Storytelling is a fundamental part of what it means to be human, and by responding to my questions out loud and leaving the recording/scribing to me, Owen was able to express these stories much more freely and articulately than he might have been able to if he was limited to written expression.

Is it possible to get the same results without an Interviewer/Scribe?

In a nutshell, no.

It's certainly possible for the essayist to make connections and ask themselves good follow-up questions—and if they respond into a recording device, they'll probably get closer to good C.A.P.E.-ready material, but a good interviewer will most certainly take the interviewee in directions the essayist would not have gone themselves.

What makes a good Interviewer/Scribe?

The good Interviewer/Scribe...

- knows the essayist
- wants the best for the essayist
- knows the importance of the **C.A.P.E.**

- prepares for the interview (by reading the prompt responses carefully, writing out questions ahead of time, noting connections, etc.)
- listens carefully
- takes great notes (or better yet, records the interview)
- doesn't limit themselves to the prepared questions (asks follow-up questions)

Memory Lane

We'll return to the prompts in a bit, but put the prompts and your responses to the side, for the time being.

By now, maybe you've already got a couple of ideas that already seem like promising starting points for your C.A.P.E. Maybe you feel like you can get moving without any more guidance. If that's the case, we're glad to know you're ready to move.

But stick with us.

We're still immersed in the information-gathering stage, and this next assignment has the potential to introduce some pretty rich material that might find its way into your **C**ollege **A**pplication **P**ersonal **E**ssay.

The Trick of Memory

Memory is a tricky thing. Prompt #7 asks, "What are your three earliest memories?" Sometimes, we confuse our earliest memories with stories that have been repeated to us by parents and older relatives.

For many years, scientists believed that human memory started at around three and a half years old. But a recent study by Carole Peterson, a memory and language researcher from Memorial University in Newfoundland, suggests that memories may start as early as two and a half years old.

This study suggests that a number of factors may account for one's ability to remember from an early age. Gender, culture, nationality, urban vs. rural home environments, how parents recall their memories, intelligence, birth order, and family size—may be included in these factors.

I include this prompt, as well as the upcoming memory assignment, because of the importance of early memories in our continued understanding of ourselves.

Leela Magavi, MD, says,

> *Early memories often align with individuals' core values, fears, hopes, and dreams. Learning about early memories can allow individuals to nurture their inner child and heal from the stressful or traumatic situations they have endured throughout their life. It can also help them gain clarity and embrace what matters the most to them.*

Given the importance of early memories, as you sit down to craft an essay through which you hope to reveal yourself to colleges, I believe it makes sense to reach out to others in an effort to urge forth stories of your early life. This C.A.P.E. Crusade Memory Assignment was created to do just that.

The C.A.P.E. Crusade Memory Assignment

In the appropriate spaces below, write the names of at least three people who have played important, significant roles in your life (friends, relatives, neighbors, family friends, teachers, siblings, babysitters, mentors, coaches, etc.).

Memory Interviewee #1	
Memory Interviewee #2	
Memory Interviewee #3	

Contact Your Memory Interviewees

When you contact your Memory Interviewees, provide them with them some version of the following statement to equip them with the appropriate context for this assignment.

Dear_____, (memory interviewee's name)

I'm preparing to write my College Application Personal Essay, and one of the pre-writing assignments I've been given is to interview three important people in my life about their memories of me.

I would greatly appreciate it if you could take a few minutes to respond to the following questions.

I can sit down with you and record your responses*, or you can record them and send me the recording. Or, if you feel like writing them out, that would also work.

If you're willing to help out with this assignment, please let me know.

Sincerely,

(Your name)

*I strongly encourage you to present your Memory Interviewees with the option to either make an audio recording of their responses or to write out their responses on paper or a Word document.

Rationale for an audio/video recording

When someone starts sharing memories, they'll reveal a great deal more if their response is recorded by audio than if you take notes with a pencil and paper. Recording their responses also allows you to listen closely and to ask follow-up questions that may help your interviewee delve further into their memories.

Rationale for reflecting in writing

Some people (I am one such person) tend to be more reflective and articulate themselves more precisely if they're given the opportunity to write out their thoughts. They feel that writing gives them a better opportunity to reflect in a measured and thoughtful manner, as well as a chance to revise their thoughts.

Memory Assignment: Interview #1

Name	
What are three words you would use to describe me when I was a child (or "when I was younger")?	
What is one of your earliest memories of me?	
What is one of your favorite memories of me?	
What is a memory you have of me that you feel speaks to an important part of my personality/ character?	
If you have heard all of these memories before, ask: What is a memory you have of me that I might not have heard before?	

Memory Assignment: Interview #2

Name	
What are three words you would use to describe me when I was a child (or "when I was younger")?	
What is one of your earliest memories of me?	
What is one of your favorite memories of me?	
What is a memory you have of me that you feel speaks to an important part of my personality/ character?	
If you have heard all of these memories before, ask: What is a memory you have of me that I might not have heard before?	

Memory Assignment: Interview #3

Name	
What are three words you would use to describe me when I was a child (or "when I was younger")?	
What is one of your earliest memories of me?	
What is one of your favorite memories of me?	
What is a memory you have of me that you feel speaks to an important part of my personality/character?	
If you have heard all of these memories before, ask: What is a memory you have of me that I might not have heard before?	

MEMORY ASSIGNMENT REFLECTION

You've just asked three important figures in your life to recall various memories they have about you. Though it's possible you've heard some or all of these stories before, as you prepare to write your College Application Personal Essay, there could be great value in examining the memories that important people in your life have of you.

As you read through or listen to your Memory Interviews, it may be very clear how you might connect and combine one or more of them to other ideas you have for your C.A.P.E. If you're not sure how you might connect them, this exercise may help.

Memory Assignment Reflection Questions

Review your interviewees' responses to the Memory Assignment and take a few minutes to respond to these questions.

Were you surprised by any of the words or memories your interviewee used to describe you?

Do the words/memories of your interviewee align with or add to your own understanding of who you are?

Do the words/memories of your interviewee seem to contradict your sense of who you are?

Which of your responses to the C.A.P.E. prompts might fit in nicely with your interviewee's responses?

Whether your interviewees' responses to the memory assignment align with, add to, or contradict your understanding of who you are, you (or someone on Team You) may find some way to connect your C.A.P.E. prompts with your Memory Interviewees' responses.

For example, one of the memories my parents always talked about in my early childhood is the time I climbed into a chair in our upstairs neighbor's apartment while she was cooking, and I simply asked, "What we gonna eat, Josie?" Both my parents claim it was the first complete sentence out of my mouth.

As it turns out, I have a deep love for cooking, eating great food, and feeding others. I could see combining that memory with my interest in the culinary arts or with my belief in the power of food to bring humans together.

I can also imagine writing an essay that combines my interest in writing and interpersonal communication, with my parents' claim that my question to Josie was my first complete sentence.

*Whether your Memory Interviewee responded to your questions digitally, in longhand (handwritten), or with an audio recording, I strongly encourage you to have a digital or hard copy of all of your material at your side for the next assignment. It might consist of notes or a complete transcription of the audio.

RETURN TO THE C.A.P.E. PROMPTS

My Life: Initial Reflections

Okay, so you've gathered anecdotes and memories. You've chronicled some of the major and minor occasions of your life, and you've reached out to three significant people in your life to tap into their memories and reflections on your life so far.

With any luck, you've returned to the table with a wealth of experiences, characters, stories, and plot points that hint at the journey you've been on for more than six thousand days.

A couple of sessions from now, we'll be encouraging you to invite others to assist you, but for now, we'd like you to take some solo time to read over, and reflect on, the materials you've gathered. These materials include your prompt responses, the memory assignment, and all the ideas you might have about this essay from before you even knew this book existed.

Whether you've responded to these prompts in digital or written form, I encourage you now to have a hard copy of them at your side.

RESPOND BEYOND ASSIGNMENT #1

Revisiting the C.A.P.E. Prompts

1. If you had to write your College Application Personal Essay right now, what do you think it would be about?
2. Look at the prompts you didn't respond to.
3. Take a moment to briefly explain why you might not have responded to them.

For example, if you didn't respond to prompt #16, return to prompt #16 in your C.A.P.E. notebook, and in the space provided, briefly explain why you didn't respond ("I couldn't think of anything to write"; "I wasn't quite ready to go there," etc.).

Note: this is not meant to push you to reveal something you do not want to reveal. The intention is dual:

    a) to give you an opportunity to reflect more deeply on the reason(s) for skipping over the prompt.

    b) to provide you a second chance to return to a prompt without being pressed for time.

4. Take some time to respond to the prompts that you skipped or did not spend enough time on.

5. Now look at the responses you wrote that were lengthier or seemed to come more easily—prompts, perhaps, that you could have written even more about. What do you think it was about these prompts that elicited that ease of reflection? Does it hint at some aspect of your character that deserves more attention? Explain.

6. Looking over your responses to the C.A.P.E. prompts, does anything else strike you as interesting or notable? Explain.

7. Does anything surprise you about your responses? Explain.

8. In navigating the world, we're trying to figure out who we are and what we stand for, and we sometimes find that we're sort of at odds with ourselves; do you notice anything in your responses that might appear contradictory? How might you explain these contradictions?

9. What are the moments that stand out to you as *defining* in some way? Or that might serve to indicate how you came to be the person you are?

10. What things about you are addressed here that will probably not be addressed elsewhere in your profile (your full application) but that you think are important for colleges to know about you?

RESPOND BEYOND ASSIGNMENT #2

Expanding the C.A.P.E. Prompts

1. Having had this chance to reflect on your prompt responses, select five that you feel say the most about you, and expand on them. Be thoughtful and thorough and self-reflective as you delve deeper into these responses.
2. Even without analysis of these documents, have any essay ideas already occurred to you? If so, take a few minutes here to jot them down.
3. If someone said you had to include five of your responses in your C.A.P.E., which five responses would you include? Do not worry about how you would connect them. Write the numbers of the prompts in your C.A.P.E. Notebook.
4. What themes, personality traits, etc., are addressed in your responses to the five prompts you selected? (e.g., family, unity, truth, honesty, communication, tenacity, civility, goodness, curiosity, growth, love, interpersonal relationships, decency, travel, history, exercise, effort, hustle, scholarship, appreciation, gratitude, justice, standing up for others.)
5. If you could only write about three of these responses in your C.A.P.E., which three would you select?
6. If you had to write your essay right now, what would you write it about?
7. Are there other things you haven't addressed here that you feel are important for colleges to know about you? If so, what are they?

Themes, Threads, and Connections

So, you've probed, mined, explored, reflected, and expanded on the prompt responses, and now it's time to reflect on the themes, motifs, and threads that invariably connect your stories.

When I work one-on-one with C.A.P.E. writers, this is where I sit down with them and read through the material they've gathered so far, with the aim of finding connections between, and among, what might at first look like distinct parts of their lives and different facets of their personalities.

Some students are particularly skilled—even gifted—at making these connections. You may have already found some of these connective tissues among your prompt responses. You might even have an idea or two about how to approach your essay.

Other students might have no idea what direction to take.

Regardless of where you find yourself in terms of making these connections, it's a good time to consider the possibility of bringing in a mentor.

The Mentor Center

It's time to find the themes, threads, and connections among your prompt responses and your memory assignment. At this point, some students already have three or four great ideas to explore for their **College App Personal Essay**. Others have no idea what direction to take. As it is with everything else in life, this part of the process comes easier to some than to others.

It's like my tennis game. I can beat most of the people I know in a tennis match, but there are countless others who could absolutely crush me at the game. It's a terrible fact.

I coached a player many years ago who ended up playing professional tennis, and when she was as young as thirteen or fourteen years old, I would hit with her before her matches. While I warmed her up, she would hit the ball right to my wheelhouse a dozen times in a row, and if you watched us, you might think, hey, he's not so bad, either. But she could (and *did*) end the point *any* time she wanted to by hitting a ball that I would *never* be able to get to.

My point is this: no matter what the skill is, there's always someone around who's better at it than we are. But this is no time to get bogged down with comparing yourself to anyone else. No one else has your stories. No one. And fortunately, you don't have to do this completely on your own.

Mentors

From Professor John Keating and his students in *Dead Poets Society* to Dumbledore and Harry Potter to Mary Poppins (mentor to Jane and Michael), to Yoda and Luke Skywalker, Hollywood movies are rich with examples of mentees and their mentors.

This may be the perfect time in the C.A.P.E. writing process to reach out to someone you might call a mentor. Even if you think you have a pretty good idea of where to go from here, it's a good idea to reach out to one. Sometimes it's just tougher to see all the possibilities; a fresh set of eyes can be just the thing you need to help you figure out an amazing direction.

And don't let the word *mentor* limit you. It doesn't have to be like Morpheus and Neo. This is a partner, an ally, a supporter, defender—someone who's on Team You.

They come in all shapes, sizes, and ages. They come equipped with all kinds of skill sets. It could be a writer, a film buff, an avid reader, an armchair psychologist, an *actual* psychologist, an amateur dream interpreter. It might be one of the people you interviewed for your memory assignment; it might be all three of them. It could be your aunt, your uncle, your mom's oldest friend.

You get the idea.

And guidance counselors, college counselors, and therapists are often great at this. I know history teachers and English teachers and lawyers, an information technology professional, a brilliant set designer, and an athletic director who would be great at this. I've found that people who love reading and talking about literature and films and philosophy and psychology and politics and big ideas are perfect partners to sit down with to review your prompt responses.

And don't neglect the possibility of talking to a trusted friend who may be the same age or even younger than you. I've had students in my English classes who were able to make mind-blowing and astute analytical observations their first time through a literary text—connections that might have taken me several readings to make (if they occurred to me at all!).

APPROACHING YOUR MENTOR/ALLY

How to approach your mentor/ally really depends on your relationship with them. With friends and relatives, a less formal approach—in person, by text, or by phone call—may be appropriate. With your grandmother who makes dates for high tea at the Palmer House, a more formal approach may be called for.

But wherever your mentor/ally lands on the spectrum of formality, you'll want to prepare them appropriately for the conversation. Writing them an email or note with some version of the following information should be enough to give them a clear sense of what you're asking of them.

You can fiddle with this approach to make it more or less formal.

CONTACTING YOUR MENTOR

I. Salutation

Dear _____

II. (Something personal regarding your connection with the person)

I hope this email finds you happy and having a good day.

III. (Update on your life)

As for me, I just finished up the school year and am looking forward to relaxing for a couple of weeks before blah, blah, blah...

IV. (Brief description of the C.A.P.E. and this assignment)

I'm currently reading a book that is guiding me through the process of writing my College Application Personal Essay. I've completed a number of assignments designed to generate ideas for my essay.

The author of the book encouraged me to sit down with someone who knows me well and might be able to help me make connections among the prompt responses and ultimately bring me closer to formulating an idea for my College Application Personal Essay.

V. (Reason you're reaching out to this person)

I think you would be a great person to do this exercise with. (You know me well, I respect your judgment, you're crazy about me, you have had insights about me that I've valued, etc.)

VI. (Request for an appointment)

I know you're busy and this might be asking a lot, but if you're available in the next week or so, I would so appreciate you sitting down with me to help me sift through this material. If life is crazy busy for you now, and you've got a lot on your plate, please don't hesitate to say so. But if you can squeeze in the time, just let me know what days and times might work for you. You can email me (phone me, text me, etc.). I look forward to hearing from you.

VII. Closing

Warmly (Sincerely, Lovingly, Love, Gratefully, etc.)

Your name

MEETING WITH YOUR MENTOR

Here are a few suggestions for that meeting with your mentor.

1) Read the prompts and your responses to your mentor. I think it's important to read the responses aloud. In hearing yourself read them, you may already begin to make connections that bring you closer to an essay idea.

2) Have an extra copy of them with you on the chance that they might like to read along with you.

3) You can also have your mentor read your responses out loud to you.

4) Invite your mentor to interrupt you throughout your reading in order to ask follow-up questions. In your elaboration of certain responses, you may make further discoveries that help you highlight connections.

Here are some additional questions for you to consider asking your mentor:

- Are there any anecdotes/responses you'd like to hear more about?
- Of all that is here, what can you imagine making its way into a personal essay?
- Do you see any interesting connections among these responses?
- Are there things about me that none of these responses seem to touch on, hint at, or address?
- Which of these responses seem to say the most about me?
- When you think of the kind of person I am, do you think of some things that I don't address in these prompt responses?

Sifting through Your Stories

So, how do you determine which anecdotes, messages, personality traits, topics, and themes should make their way into your College Application Personal Essay?

Whether or not the direction of your C.A.P.E. already seems clear to you, these next two exercises were designed to help you sift through the stories you've curated so far to help determine the direction of your essay.

Assignment #1

With your prompt responses at your side, read the following questions, and in the blank spaces that follow, write the numbers of the prompts that respond appropriately to the question.

1. Which prompt responses speak to my personality, my life as a thinking, feeling, interesting human being?				
#	#	#	#	#
#	#	#	#	#

2. Which prompt responses are funny?				
#	#	#	#	#
#	#	#	#	#

3. Which prompt responses are interesting?				
#	#	#	#	#
#	#	#	#	#

4. Which prompt responses are meaningful?				
#	#	#	#	#
#	#	#	#	#

5. Which prompt responses hint at my passion for something?				
#	#	#	#	#
#	#	#	#	#

6. Which prompt responses speak to the way I live?				
#	#	#	#	#
#	#	#	#	#

7. Which prompt responses feel genuine and honest?				
#	#	#	#	#
#	#	#	#	#

8. Which prompt responses contain more than one layer of meaning?				
#	#	#	#	#
#	#	#	#	#

9. Which prompt responses contain more than one emotion in the layers of this story?				
#	#	#	#	#
#	#	#	#	#

10. Which prompt responses are deeply truthful?

#	#	#	#	#
#	#	#	#	#

11. Which prompt responses are compelling?

#	#	#	#	#
#	#	#	#	#

12. Which prompt responses are inspiring or uplifting?

#	#	#	#	#
#	#	#	#	#

13. Which prompt responses speak to a limitation, mistake, or regret?

#	#	#	#	#
#	#	#	#	#

14. Which prompt responses contain a lesson that has shaped me? Informed me? Helped me to grow?

#	#	#	#	#
#	#	#	#	#

15. Which prompt responses have led me to deep self-reflection?

#	#	#	#	#
#	#	#	#	#

16. Which prompt responses speak to me as a growing, unfolding, developing person?				
#	#	#	#	#
#	#	#	#	#

17. Which prompt responses are singular? Unique? Distinguish me from others?				
#	#	#	#	#
#	#	#	#	#

18. Which prompt responses speak to something universal about humans?				
#	#	#	#	#
#	#	#	#	#

19. Which prompt responses tell a good story?				
#	#	#	#	#
#	#	#	#	#

Assignment #2

Respond appropriately to the following.

1) In the left-hand column below, write the numbers of the prompts that come up most often in the previous assignment.

2) In the right-hand column, write the theme (or themes) you would assign to the prompt in the left column (e.g., family, unity, truth, honesty, curiosity, hustle, etc.).

Prompt	Theme(s)
#	
#	
#	
#	
#	
#	
#	
#	
#	
#	

3) What themes come up most often in #2 above?

4) Which of these themes are most critical to understanding you?

5) What two or three themes would you most like to work into your essay? (Don't worry yet about *how* to work them in).

It may be pretty clear to you which of your responses to the prompts might make it into your essay. At this point, it's important not to be too critical about your responses. That time you fought with a kindergarten classmate over the affection of another classmate might not seem like it has all-star essay potential, but if it connects with one or two other prompt responses, it still might make the cut.

And don't feel bad about taking a marker and putting a giant X through the prompt responses that you don't want to explore any further, for whatever reasons.

THREAD-LESS AND DISCONNECTED? (HAVE NO FEAR)

If you don't see the threads, themes, and connections...

Now that you're more aware of the purpose of the C.A.P.E. prompts, it might be worthwhile to look at them again, pressing yourself to deeper reflection.

Take another look at page 44 where I provided a long list of essay topics. Think of these topics as another kind of prompting. For example, if you were asked to write a letter to your younger self, let's say, to prepare your eighth-grade self for the next four years, what would be a few things you'd have to say?

Which of the topics can you now imagine as a topic for your C.A.P.E.?

Take a close look at your prompt responses. Imagine that you're reading a book, one chapter of which is a bullet point list of the protagonist's responses to these exact prompts. Pretend there's a bit of dramatic irony going on—which is to say, the protagonist doesn't know as much about their own life as you do. Or maybe they're a little hard-headed and just don't want to see what they're made of. What would you say about a character like this? What notes would you make in the margins of each of the responses?

On the chance that you're *still* coming up threadless, themeless, connectionless...

When I work one-on-one with students who take the online or face-to-face C.A.P.E. Crusader Course, it's not uncommon to come across students whose prompt responses barely scratch the surface of who they are.

Some students are more private than others. Some students are understandably reluctant to delve too deeply into difficult or emotionally charged stories and events. I can't begin to address the infinity of reasons why this is a more difficult endeavor for some students than for others, but I get it.

It's probably a good time to remind you that the College Application Personal Essay isn't asking you to reveal your deepest and most emotionally charged stories. Again, the C.A.P.E. is merely asking you to tell us a bit about who you are, if you're likely to thrive on a college campus, and if you're ready for college writing. That's all.

And not finding any connections or threads doesn't necessarily mean that something's wrong, that you're on your way to writing a terrible essay, or that you're not willing to dig deep. It could also mean there's more to you than you think. If every prompt urges forth some different facet of your life and your personality, maybe a montage essay is the way for you to go.

If you think this might be the case, take another close look at your prompt responses. Responding to the following questions might help you make some connections you hadn't thought of otherwise.

Montage Essay Assignment

- Write the number of the prompts to which you feel most connected.
- Why do you feel most connected to them?
- Which responses do you feel are essential to understanding you?
- Why do you feel this way?
- Underline your favorite anecdotes.
- Why are they your favorite anecdotes?
- Think of a symbol, an object, or a word for your response to every prompt and draw it/write it in the margin next to your response. If you had a photo album that had one photo for each response, what would that photograph look like?
- Now, in the margins of your prompt responses, assign a value, or a number of values, to each of your responses. For example: family, unity, truth, honesty, communication, tenacity, civility, goodness, curiosity, growth, love, interpersonal relationships, decency, travel, history, exercise, effort, hustle, scholarship, appreciation, gratitude, justice, standing up for others, alone time.

After this exercise, you might have enough material for a list or a montage essay, which we'll cover in a subsequent session.

Pantsers and Plotters (Or, to Outline or Not to Outline)

There are writers who swear by outlines and writers who swear *at* them. The former group—those who plan out their writing, are sometimes called "plotters." And the latter group—writers who swear *at* the idea of outlines—are called "pantsers," because they write "by the seat of their pants."

Every writer can be placed somewhere on the Outline User Spectrum.

Outline User Spectrum

Never Use (Pantsers)   Always Use (Plotters)

I'm not much of a plotter, for the most part. I've got a pretty good innate sense of how a critical essay, short story, or short*ish* creative nonfiction essay should be organized. But when it comes to longer-form stuff—long essays, novels, long short stories, plays, and screenplays—I feel a little more grounded if I've got an outline to work from.

An important distinction to make, though, is that even if I outline a piece before I sit down to the actual writing, I *always* leave the door open for discovery. I'll address this point more deliberately in my attention to the *discovery draft* below.

But make no mistake about it; organization is important for this essay. There are an infinite number of ways to write a **C**ollege **A**pplication **P**ersonal **E**ssay, but every reader of every college essay wants to see the logic in the organization. And one of the easiest ways to lose a reader is by giving them an essay that's like one of those skinny balloons that take an hour to blow up and then dart away from you and zoom around the room without any organizing principle.

Bottom line: your C.A.P.E. needs organization. It needs a logical narrative structure. You can have an outline in your head or an outline on paper before you sit down, or you can wait until you've got an early draft complete. But organization is critical.

A couple of things to think about:

- If you're an outliner and have always been one, I wouldn't change now. Start with an outline.
- If you've never been an outliner but feel it's important to begin this important essay with an outline, you can consider it.
- But if you think an outline might keep you from making the important discoveries that will come with a more free-wheeling, free-thinking, free-writing early draft—by all means, tackle this *discovery draft* without an outline.
- In any case, I think it makes sense to have some idea of what a basic outline for a **C**ollege **A**pplication **P**ersonal **E**ssay might look like before you begin writing. It's important to note, though, that there is room for flexibility here; every essay deserves its own outline. If you use one of the two sample outlines provided here as a guide, you won't go wrong.

OUTLINE EXAMPLES

Below are outlines for two successful essays that appear in the addendum. I call them the *Stay Upper* and the *Tapping In* essays. The outlines are also presented in the addendum in slightly greater depth. They're not meant to be templates, but they can be modified for many types of essays.

Lucy's Stay-Upper Essay Outline

I. Hook: an interesting story to pull the reader in immediately. It might be funny, surprising, unexpected, powerful, or even ridiculous.

II. Brief explanation of what it means to be a *stay upper*.

III. Extends the idea of what it means to be a stay upper, to be a full participant in all of life, from the ordinary to the extraordinary moments.

IV. Body of the essay: A recent experience that represents the full embodiment of what it means to be a stay upper.

V. Closer: Some kind of return, however brief, to the stay-upper hook.

Cole's Tapping-In Essay Outline

I. Hook: an interesting story to pull the reader in immediately. It might be funny, surprising, unexpected, powerful, even ridiculous.

II. Brief history of essayist playing in a band with his father.

III. Essayist introduces his growing interest but lack of confidence in taking over his father's role as the guitar soloist on stage. He finally taps on his father's shoulder to take over the solo.

IV. Body of the essay: essayist extends the idea of "tapping in" to suggest complete participation in social, academic, and extracurricular arenas.

V. Closer: A brief return to the moment on stage when the essayist taps on his father's shoulder to take on the guitar solo.

CHAPTER 3

Discovery and Access

I call Chapter Three "Discovery and Access" to call attention to what are arguably the most important elements of your College Application Personal Essay: 1) finding your way into the C.A.P.E. and 2) making the discoveries necessary to give shape to the great essay that you have simmering within.

So far, you've made your way through three of the four primary challenges of the college essay process.

1) Pulling together the important stories of your life

2) Sifting through and reflecting on the importance of your stories

3) Selecting the most striking, revealing, and significant stories

The remaining challenge is the last of them: 4) Presenting your story effectively in a 650-word essay.

This part may be the trickiest. My hope is that breaking it down into its various components may help in facing the toughest part.

There are two major elements to Challenge #4: a) building the discovery draft, and b) sculpting the discovery draft into the final 650-word masterpiece.

THE C.A.P.E. PROCESS

Challenge #4: Presenting your story effectively in a 650-word essay

Part I. Building the Discovery Draft

1. The Access Intro: Finding Your Way In
2. A Word about Word Count
3. Ignoring Your Inner Editor...
4. Getting Started on the Discovery Draft

Part II. From the Discovery Draft to the Final Draft

- Revisiting
- Revising

The Discovery Draft

Few essayists know exactly what it is they want to say before they explore the idea long enough to write it with any kind of beauty or precision or impact. The word *essay,* in fact, comes from the French word *essais,* meaning to try, to attempt, to test.

Many years ago, I stopped using the term "first draft" to speak about the earliest draft of essays or stories. I now use the term *discovery draft.*

Discovery draft speaks to the importance of our earliest efforts at putting language to the thing within. One of the most brilliant thinkers and writers I know feels he can't grasp much of anything without first putting down his thoughts in writing. And much of the joy in writing comes from making these discoveries.

Later in this course, I'll address the importance of a good, strong opening, but if the earliest efforts of a story are about *discovery,* it takes the pressure of the opening off of you (for now).

This is why Anne Lamott, in her book *Bird by Bird,* has a chapter called "'Crappy' First Drafts" (*Crappy* is in quotation marks because Lamott actually uses another word for "crappy")

Along those same lines, the writer John Green says this of the earliest drafts of new material:

> *I just give myself permission to suck. I delete about 90 percent of my first drafts…so it doesn't really matter much if on a particular day I write beautiful and brilliant prose that will stick in the minds of my readers forever, because there's a 90 percent chance*

I'm just gonna delete whatever I write anyway. I find this hugely liberating.

So, what does this mean for you when you sit down to the discovery draft of your C.A.P.E.?

All of the sessions in Chapter 3 were developed with the guiding principle of *discovery* in mind. It's the reason I don't want you to be concerned about any of the elements of the final draft that might hold you back in the early stages. I don't want you to be concerned about word count, spelling, grammar, punctuation, organization, the introduction and conclusion, etc.

This is your opportunity to write thoughtfully, reflectively, and extensively about anything and everything that has come to the surface through the pre-writing you've just done.

Even if you feel you already have some sense of how your essay is going to begin, unfold, and end, it's important that you do all you can to allow discovery to take place. The thing about discovery is that you never know what you'll come across.

The Access Intro: Finding Your Way In

As writers spend more time writing at the table, more time developing, growing, reading, and practicing their craft, their early drafts get better and better.

But this certainty remains: if we've convinced you that our earliest writing efforts are about *exploration* and *discovery*, it should take some of the anxiety from the pressure of the opening line.

All we need to do is find a way *in*. All we need is *access* to the essay.

I coined the term **access intro** after years of noting a common trait in the creative and critical writing of my high school students. The essays very often seem to end in places other than the author seemed to suggest in their introduction.

Let's look at an example in the arena of the critical essay. A student reads *The Great Gatsby* and decides to write his essay on the symbolism of the green light glowing from the deck of Daisy Buchanan's house. He plans to connect the green light with Gatsby's dream of being with Daisy Buchanan. In the opening paragraph, he begins to establish Daisy's character and latches onto the narrator's description of Daisy's voice. As he continues writing, he finds several more instances of Nick Carraway's (the narrator) description of Daisy's voice, and by the third paragraph, he believes he has found some compelling evidence that the narrator, himself, seems to have a crush on his cousin, Daisy Buchanan. Our hypothetical student continues in this surprising and brilliant direction, finishes the essay that has been hanging over his head for weeks, and, immensely pleased with himself, imagines the mind-blown face of his teacher as she reads his genius essay. The author taps the printed essay on his desk like a deck of cards, staples it, makes himself a late-night grilled cheese, and hands in the essay the next day.

When the teacher finally gets to grading the essay, she reads the author's introduction, thinking she's going to read yet another essay about the green light, but when she gets to her student's concluding paragraph, she reads:

Nearly every young reader of *The Great Gatsby* thinks of F. Scott Fitzgerald's masterpiece as a love story—and it is. But it is not the story of Gatsby's love for his old flame; rather, it is the story of Nick Carraway's love for his husky-voiced cousin, Daisy Buchanan.

Like so many apprentice writers, the Gatsby essayist has an aversion to revision. Because they have not yet realized the importance and art of *revision*, they failed to understand the greatest value of the first draft: discovery, and so they also failed to see the first-draft introduction for what it is: an *opportunity* to provide them *access* to the discovery draft. Nothing more. The only responsibility of the first-draft introduction is to help you *find your way into* the discovery draft.

The Access Intro of the C.A.P.E., then, is whatever you have to do to get the essay started. Do whatever you have to do to find access to your story. If "once upon a time" is enough to get you started, have at it.

A Word about Word Count

Let's think about the first draft as a discovery vessel at sea, intended to drag the ocean floor for information that the discoverers hope will help them learn the story of the ocean.

The captain, and sole crew member of the vessel, has been given the task of coming back with ocean floor samples. The ship can take on more than 5000 pounds of samples while it's at sea but must return to shore with no more than 650 lbs. of ocean samples.

Captain Word Count, a messy-haired, hard-headed fellow nearly eighteen years of age, has a rich life outside of this maritime work, and he doesn't want to spend the entire summer scraping the ocean bottom, so he decides, forthwith, to drag the ocean only until he scoops up his 650-pound limit, which, as it turns out, is met after he rakes up a solitary scoop just a nautical city block offshore.

Our point, of course, is that Captain Word Count should not be steering the ship this early in the game. He'll never be able to tell the history of the ocean if all he's thinking about is the 650-pound limit assigned to him.

I can't express this enough. Please don't worry about the word count. Don't even think about it.

As we've said before, the earliest draft of your College Application Personal Essay is a *discovery draft*. This essay represents the greatest amount of control you have over your application at this point, and you don't want to hand over that power by fettering yourself with something as trivial as the number of words you're allotted.

This is not the time to give a second of thought to word count. Give yourself time and space to explore the depth and breadth of your eighteen years of history—that's about six thousand days of life!

I hope that I've convinced you by now that *discovery* is the goal of the first draft. And discovery is going to be impossible, or at the very least, profoundly limited, if you start thinking of word count too soon.

Obsess over word count now, and I guarantee that you'll never get to the discoveries necessary for a great essay.

Imagine that you're secretly competing with your classmates to write a ten-thousand-word discovery draft. If you come back to shore with more than ten thousand words, we'll sift through the flotsam and jetsam and worry about the word count later.

Ignoring Your Inner Editor and Other Things Not to Worry about (For Now)

Talk to hundreds of writers about their writing process, and you're likely to hear a thousand processes for writing.

There are writers who edit as they go, writers who free write and never cross out a line until they finish a full draft, writers who write out one paragraph to a page and make sure every word is perfect before they move on to the next paragraph, writers who think out a project for two years before putting a single word to a page, and writers who change their process for every new writing project.

As I mentioned early on, my own writing process includes writing the discovery draft longhand with my Palomino *Blackwing 602* in my National Brand Chemistry Notebook (Item No. 43-571). I think of myself as a casual editor as I go along. I leave ample room in the left margin of the notebook to take notes and write thoughts I might get to later when I start the real editing process, and I rarely erase. I draw a single line through the words I want to strike, just in case I might want to get back to them.

But even if you've got a writing process that has never let you down, unless you're very comfortable writing personal essays, you may find that your methodology might not work for this particular essay.

The discovery draft may be particularly problematic for you if you've got one of those nasty inner editors who doesn't let you move on to the second sentence until the first sentence is perfect.

As much as possible, I encourage you to shut up that inner editor. Shut it up and shut it down. Forget about seamless transitions, forget about an architecturally exquisite structure, forget about gorgeous sentences and brilliant syntax.

Your campaign, in the earliest stages of the actual writing of this essay, is to get everything down on paper. Write, write, write. Forget about word count, ignore your inner editor, and shush your inner critic. There's no place for them here. This is a no-judgment zone.

If something strikes you as an even remotely important anecdote, explore it by writing about it.

Getting Started on the Discovery Draft, or JSW (Just Start Writing)

Whether you've been working in your C.A.P.E. notebook or on your laptop, hopefully you've equipped yourself with more than enough material—the *stuff* of your life—to create one of the most important documents of your young life.

And in this *resource material*, let's call it, you've inevitably discovered threads, themes, and connections, and maybe you've got three or four ideas you're thinking about working into your essay—maybe you've got closer to a dozen.

Wherever you are with those anecdotes, it doesn't matter.

Just start writing.

Maybe you've got a paragraph's worth of writing for each of them; maybe it's only a sentence.

Just start writing.

Take each of the prompts, take your memory assignment, and take your mentor's thoughts about them, too, and starting one paragraph at a time, write as much as you can about that memory, that photograph, that anecdote, that story. Get all the mileage you can out of it. Reflect more on it. Write some more. Why is it an important story? What values can you assign to it? What did it teach you? How did it inform your understanding of the world? How did it shape you? How did it make you see the world differently? How was it a watershed moment for you? Did the experience make you want to be a different person? Did it turn you in the direction of a career? A new mindset? A different way of seeing the world?

When you've exhausted the possibilities, move on to the next anecdote, the next prompt, the next memory, and do the same thing. Don't worry just yet about transitions and perfect mechanics and spelling. Don't worry about creating an unforgettable opening sentence and a powerful conclusion. And *please, please, please* don't worry about word count. It's still too early.

As you're writing, think about the previous prompts you've extended into paragraphs. Can you feel the connections growing? If you can't, don't worry about it. The important thing is that everything you write—every prompt you expand, every discovery you make while writing and thinking and reflecting—says something about who you are and helps you come closer to presenting your true self.

This page is blank (sort of), and the next page is totally blank because they're symbolic of . . .

You writing the discovery draft of your C.A.P.E.

(Also, you're not thinking about word count.)

[Intentional blank page]

CHAPTER 4
Putting Shape to Your C.A.P.E.

Okay. You've got something. Maybe it feels like there's even a beginning, middle, and end.

Despite our insistence to ignore word count, there's something about it that's really hard to ignore. About 70 percent of the students I work with end up with discovery drafts that clock in within a few hundred words of the 650-word limit.

Doesn't matter. Wherever you're at with it, hopefully, you've made some discoveries and have landed upon a story or two that speak to who you are, and you've got a discovery draft you can work with.

Now we begin part two of the final challenge of the C.A.P.E.: moving from the discovery draft to the final draft.

I'm not going to lie. This may be the toughest part of the C.A.P.E. process. In my work as a C.A.P.E. coach, shaping the essay is the point at which most college applicants reach out to members of my staff and me for one-on-one coaching assistance.

In the next sections, I'll provide you with material and suggestions to help you successfully approach this critical stage of the College Application Personal Essay process.

Revisiting the Discovery Draft

Over the next few pages, I'll expand on the following suggestions to help you bring your C.A.P.E. closer to the final draft.

1) Set your discovery draft aside for a day or two (or three or four)
2) Re-read your discovery draft
3) Retrofit an outline to your discovery draft
4) Compare your resource material with your discovery draft

SET YOUR DISCOVERY DRAFT ASIDE

In Chapter 3, I encouraged you to ignore your inner editor and just write. Just letting the words flow—without concern for things like punctuation, word count, tone, diction, syntax, and transitions—can lead writers to discoveries they might not make when they feel fettered by the conventions and rules and boundaries that we often associate with formal writing assignments.

If you took my suggestion to ignore your inner editor, it's quite possible that your discovery draft is a bit of a mess. Maybe you got into a fluid writing zone and went in a dozen directions that are now in need of rethinking.

Undoubtedly, there are also errors in grammar and spelling. Or maybe you ended up writing on a theme about which you didn't actually intend on writing, and it now needs reorganization.

Setting aside your discovery draft will give you a much-needed opportunity to put some distance between you and your C.A.P.E. So take a break. Go for a run, watch a movie, make a smoothie, listen to some music, take a nap, have a catch, shoot some hoops, make a grilled cheese sandwich, and come back to the essay with a fresh perspective.

The *you* who sat down to write the discovery draft is different from the *you* who is going to sit down after your break. And the new *you* needs to believe in this essay, too.

RE-READ YOUR DISCOVERY DRAFT

You're actually only reading your essay for the first time here, but I use the term "re-reading" because it includes three steps:

1) The first reading: reading it to yourself
2) The second reading: reading it out loud
3) The third reading: having someone else read it to you

The first reading: read it to yourself

Your purpose in this first reading is not necessarily to proofread. Of course, you can fix spelling errors and correct mechanical mistakes, but it's still too early for fine-tuning. The larger point is to *revisit* the C.A.P.E. with the purpose of strengthening it, infusing it with more of *you*.

So, ask yourself these questions as you read your discovery draft:

- If an admissions officer read this discovery draft just as it is, how might he/she/they think of me as a student on their college campus?
- Would they have a sense of my personality?
- Would they see me as a student who could thrive on their college campus?

- Would they be excited about what I might add to their school?

The second reading: read it out loud

Sometimes, reading your work out loud—as though you were reading to an audience—allows you to imagine more clearly how others might *receive* the essay. You'll catch mistakes, of course, but you'll also begin to think more realistically about your audience.

The third reading: have someone else read it to you

Ask a friend or relative you trust to read your essay out loud to you. When we read our own work, we know what we meant to say, and so we might not see certain imprecisions or mistakes. When someone else reads your work out loud, they will be less likely to ignore moments that lack clarity and precision. They will be more likely to call attention to anything that seems amiss.

RETROFIT AN OUTLINE TO
YOUR DISCOVERY DRAFT

Whether you sat down to write your discovery draft with an outline or not, retrofitting an outline to your discovery draft (or reverse outlining) is intended to help you objectively evaluate the work you've completed so far by looking at the organization of the draft you've written.

How to retrofit an outline to your discovery draft

Read one paragraph at a time to determine the main idea of each paragraph. Write the idea in the margins of the essay. If there are multiple ideas in the paragraph, note them all in the margins.

Ask yourself the following questions as you look at each of the paragraphs:

- What is the point I want to get across in this paragraph?
- Is it an essential point?
- Did I make the point?
- Is it clear?
- Can I make it clearer?
- Is there more than one main idea in the paragraph?
- Are there many main ideas?
- Is the campaign of the paragraph clear?
- Do I repeat myself in this paragraph?
- How does this paragraph connect to my greater point?

COMPARE YOUR RESOURCE MATERIAL WITH YOUR DISCOVERY DRAFT

This is critical.

One of the great frustrations for many of my students at this point is that they feel they put a lot of thought into their responses to their prompts and their memory assignment, but they still feel their discovery draft doesn't present them as they are.

The purpose of this suggestion is to take a close look at your discovery draft and stack what it says about you against what your other resource materials say about you.

Your resources materials include your prompt responses, your expanded responses, your memory assignment, and anything else you've brought to the table prior to picking up this book.

Ask yourself these questions as you compare your discovery draft with your resource material:

- If an admissions officer read my prompts, which of them would they probably want to hear more about?
- What interesting, notable things about me are included in my resources but are not included in my discovery draft (but probably should be)?

After you've revisited the discovery draft and have taken these suggestions into account, you should be ready to take another shot at your C.A.P.E.

Two Common (and Flawed) Approaches to the First Draft of the C.A.P.E.

I mentioned above that many college application personal essayists reach out to me for help at this point. Very often, it's because their discovery draft doesn't quite present them as the person they see themselves to be. My hope is that looking at two flawed approaches to the first draft of the College Application Personal Essay may help illustrate a common frustration of essayists at this point.

You'll notice first that the title above ("Two Common (and flawed) Approaches to the First Draft of the C.A.P.E.") uses the term *first draft* instead of *discovery draft*. This is deliberate. One of the real frustrations occurs here because essayists often have an essay topic in mind from the start, and they write the essay they have been thinking of for months. There's nothing inherently wrong with that, unless the draft ignores essential discoveries that can really deepen and enrich the essay.

COMMON (AND FLAWED) ESSAY TOPIC #1: THE COMMUNITY SERVICE ESSAY

Every year, I read first drafts of essays that focus on community service work. The types of volunteer work vary, of course, but the typical community service essay can be summarized something like this:

There's a collection of tents under Lake Shore Drive, where dozens of homeless people live. When I turned ten, I decided to do something to help them. I asked everyone who attended my birthday party to bring blankets, socks, and toiletries instead of presents, and I distributed the items to the homeless people who live there. This experience has made me realize how many people

117

are homeless in the country and how we need to help them as much as we can.

So, what's flawed about this community service essay?

It's common

Perhaps the greatest weakness of these essays is that they're common in multiple ways: the topic is common, the meaning is barely skin-deep, and the writing is common. The problem with this essay is that many college applicants think their essays should say something about their concern for others, and a very common way for them to do this is by writing about their service to the community.

It doesn't do more than one thing

The essay only speaks about the student's service to the homeless community. It doesn't speak to any other aspects of the student's life.

It doesn't move beyond other elements in the student profile

The essay is an opportunity to show who the student is beyond other elements of their student profile. The section of the profile that includes the extracurricular activities of the student should mention their community service. This essay doesn't move beyond the student's resume.

It could come across as trite and vague

It's overused, lacks originality, and it can carry a tone of privilege.

So, should you not write a community service essay?

It's important to note that there's not anything wrong with the community service essay *topic*. I have read many *good* and some *great* essays on community service, but the great community service essays go far beyond the simple act of service.

COMMON (AND FLAWED) ESSAY TOPIC #2: THE VOLUNTOURISM ESSAY

Voluntourism is a *portmanteau* (a word created from a blending of two or more words) of volunteer and tourism. It's a form of tourism in which travelers visit a place and combine their visit with volunteer work. The typical voluntourism essay can be summarized something like this:

I went on a service trip to San Juan, Texas, after junior year, where we helped build houses for migrant farm workers. While we were there we stayed in the homes of extremely poor people from San Juan. The family I stayed with barely had anything; they lived in a tin shack with chickens in the yard and showers that ran only cold water, but they seemed so happy. And what they did have, they were very generous with. They cooked our meals, and the parents insisted that I sleep in their room while they slept in their children's room. It really showed me how hospitable they were, and how happy people could be even if they have almost nothing. It really gave me an appreciation for all that I have.

So, what's wrong with the voluntourism essay?

119

Voluntourism receives an ever-growing share of heavy criticism

Despite the best intentions underpinning *voluntourism* and its positive benefits, voluntourism also has many critics. A quick internet search for "criticisms of voluntourism" reveals many such complaints about voluntourism.

Essays on volunteer trips often hint more at privilege than service

One of the reasons that voluntourism continues to grow in popularity is that it's a multi-billion-dollar industry. It depends on tourists who can pay a lot of money to travel abroad to participate in this work. And so, a reader of the common voluntourism essay can walk away from the essay knowing little more about the essayist than that they're privileged.

The voluntourism essay could also come across as trite and vague

As is the case with the common community service essay, the common voluntourism essay can also lack originality and freshness.

So, should you not write an essay on a volunteer trip abroad?

As I said about the community service essay, there's nothing inherently wrong with the voluntourism topic, either. You simply need to avoid the pitfalls.

MOVING BEYOND THE COMMON

But students who write their College Application Personal Essays on community service and voluntourism simply *have* to move beyond the common.

The great community service and volunteer trip essays address the depth and reach of the impact of the service done. They suggest a great deal more about the interaction of the student and the community served. In many of these essays, nothing suggests much about the interaction with the population served. The volunteer in the first essay summary held a blanket, socks, and toiletry drive and merely distributed the items to the homeless people who lived under Lake Shore Drive. The voluntourist interacted more with the people of San Juan, but their reflection didn't go far beneath the surface.

In the next session, we'll provide some questions to help you dig a little deeper.

Digging Deep

Here are some questions I think will help you determine if your discovery draft needs a major overhaul.

1. What aspect(s) of your character or personality does the essay highlight?
2. How has the occasion, story, or event changed you in a positive way?
3. Are you satisfied that the essay shows the reader who you are?
4. Does the essay suggest how you will interact with others?
5. Will the essay distinguish you from the rest of the applicant pool?
6. What are other aspects of your personality that this essay does not address?

Now, let's move on to the revision.

Re-Vision

Only one writer I know of has ever said he doesn't revise his work. He's either the most brilliant writer on the planet or he's lying.

I began to understand the value of revising when a writing teacher urged me to think of revision as a hyphenated phrase—*re-vision*. It helped me to think of revision as a new way of seeing the writing project.

This section on re-vision was designed to impress upon you the absolute necessity of reviewing, reexamining, and reassessing the discovery draft you have built from the stories that have shaped you. The process of re-vision is intended to help you bring your C.A.P.E. to its best self.

THE INTRODUCTION AND THE CONCLUSION: PRIMACY AND RECENCY

Ask nearly any novelist, short story author, playwright, or songwriter what the most difficult part of their work is, and the chances are pretty good they'll say something about the introduction or the conclusion.

If you've taken our encouragement to not worry about fine-tuning your essay through the early stages of the writing process, then it's a good time to begin thinking more deeply about the precise wording of two very important elements of the College Application Personal Essay: the introduction and conclusion.

There's a theory called the *primacy and recency effect* that's addressed in academic disciplines ranging from psychology to education to communication. But the theory is also at play in virtually every writing project, from Post-it notes you leave on the refrigerator to iPhone texts to emails to poetry to business letters, love letters, articles, essays, and novels.

Simply stated, the *primacy and recency effect* (or theory) suggests that the things we remember best are the first and last things we're presented with.

What this means for the C.A.P.E. is that you want to have a good, strong, powerful, and effective introduction, and you want to have a good, strong, powerful, and effective conclusion.

In the next two sections, we'll look closely at a few ways to inject energy into your introduction and conclusion.

PRIMACY: THE C.A.P.E. INTRODUCTION

In the previous section, I mentioned that writers across all genres argue that the introduction and the conclusion are often the two most challenging parts of their work.

For college essayists, I would argue that it's the introduction that presents the greatest challenge. If every sentence carries the responsibility of pulling the reader into the next sentence, it's hard to overestimate the importance of the introduction.

How often are we reminded of the importance of the great opening to a story?

The poetry editor of a highly respected literary magazine once told me that when he has a stack of poems to get through for a particular issue, he gives a poem *five* lines before either rejecting it or continuing to read it for further consideration.

He added that with his five-line policy, he was one of the more generous editors in the poetry world; many of his counterparts around the country gave a poem three lines or less. If something beautiful or brilliant (or both) wasn't happening in the poem by then, the editors put the poem in the rejection pile.

We can extend that thinking to prose as well, and though the admissions team reading your **C**ollege **A**pplication **P**ersonal **E**ssay is likely to be more forgiving than editors at the *New Yorker*, suffice it to say that the goal of your opening is to get the reader wanting more.

Here are some unforgettable opening lines from great works of fiction.

"You better not never tell nobody but God."
The Color Purple, Alice Walker

"It was a bright cold day in April, and the
clocks were striking thirteen."
1984, George Orwell

"I am an invisible man."
Invisible Man, Ralph Ellison

"Ships at a distance have every man's wish on board."
Their Eyes Were Watching God, Zora Neale Hurston

"This is the saddest story I have ever heard."
The Good Soldier, Ford Madox Ford

"Mother died today. Or maybe yesterday, I don't know."
The Stranger, Albert Camus

"Stella, cold, cold, the coldness of hell."
The Shawl, Cynthia Ozick

"They shoot the white girl first."
Beloved, Toni Morrison

"I have never begun a novel with more misgiving."
The Razor's Edge, Somerset Maugham

"I was born twice: first, as a baby girl, on a remarkably smogless Detroit day in January of 1960; and then again, as a teenage boy, in an emergency room near Petoskey, Michigan, in August of 1974."
Middlesex, Jeffrey Eugenides

"Many years later, as he faced the firing squad, Colonel Aureliano Buendía was to remember that distant afternoon when his father took him to discover ice."
One Hundred Years of Solitude, Gabriel García Márquez

As you might conclude from these openings, there are no steadfast rules for the opening lines of fiction. It's safe to say, though, that there are at least three qualities of an effective opening:

1) It's a hook, an attention-getter, memorable

2) It pulls the reader into the story

3) It does more than one thing

Do More than One Thing

Let's take the first two qualities of the opening for granted. We can say these two things about every opening listed above: they're attention-getters, and they pull the reader into the story.

We can also say with great confidence that you want the same for the opening of your C.A.P.E. You want it to be memorable and to pull the reader into the essay.

This third quality—do more than one thing—doesn't stipulate what things the opening does; it merely states that it should do more than one thing. Among other things, it can announce themes, struggles, conditions, characters, drama, tone, voice, and narrative point of view.

That's all you have to do when you're writing fiction? Create an unforgettable, attention-grabbing opening that gets the reader wanting more? That's a lot to expect from an opening.

But it's important to note that these stunning opening lines you come across in your reading of great stories and novels are rarely the authors' first efforts at the opening. To read them here may make it seem easy, but the introduction is very often the most worked-over, rewritten, revised, revisited part of the story, novel, play, poem, or essay. In other words, most of the work of the introduction is painstaking work done in the revision process.

In a subsequent section of the C.A.P.E. Crusade, I'll present you with a sample outline that opens with the following sentence:

"My name is Lucy, and deep down, I'm what I've been since I was six years old. I'm a stay upper."

What I like about this opening is that it **does more than one thing**.

It's unexpected.

It's humorous in that it's almost like the opening for a statement from someone who's in a support group for *stay uppers*.

It hints at a character trait that marks the essayist's personality.

127

It pulls the reader in, because it's childlike and the term is probably unfamiliar to them.

In short, I think the reader is enticed and ready to read on.

The Access Intro, A Reminder

In an earlier session, I spoke of the sole responsibility of the *access intro* to the C.A.P.E. Namely, it is simply to get you started—to give you *access* to your **C**ollege **A**pplication **P**ersonal **E**ssay. But unless you hit the college essay lottery, that access intro is very unlikely to remain the opening of the final draft of your C.A.P.E.

Now is the time to look back at your access intro and consider what you might do to pack it with the power and punch to pull the reader into the essay, to leave your reader with something to remember, and to see that it does more than one thing.

Here's another opening from one of our C.A.P.E. participants:

> *When I walked out late for kindergarten recess that day, my closest friends were standing on the big jagged rocks that bordered the pit in the back of the playground. Becky, who was standing on the largest boulder, yelled out my name and said, "You are being put on trial for not swimming with me today."*

Does it hook you as a reader? Does it do more than one thing? Does it pull you in and make you want to continue reading? Do you wonder about the path the author is going to take you on?

There's a good chance that the work you've already done to this point may have produced a couple of great opening lines, but if you'd like to take a look at more C.A.P.E. openings, simply do an internet search for college essay openings.

RECENCY: THE C.A.P.E. CONCLUSION

I stated earlier that nearly every novelist, short story author, playwright, or songwriter speaks about the introduction and the conclusion as two of the most challenging elements of their work.

Fortunately, you're not writing a story, a play, a novel, or a song. And for a number of reasons, I would argue that the conclusion of the **C**ollege **A**pplication **P**ersonal **E**ssay presents fewer challenges than the introduction.

For one, the conclusion doesn't bear the responsibility of bringing you to the next line. By the time you reach the conclusion, you've already done the heavy lifting of bringing the reader to the end of the essay.

The conclusion is an opportunity to tie the essay together. Though we often don't want our stories and novels and plays to reach a conclusion that neatly and tidily ties everything together, it's quite all right for our college essays to do just that. But it doesn't have to.

A widely accepted guiding principle for the conclusion of the **C**ollege **A**pplication **P**ersonal **E**ssay is simply that it returns, however briefly, to the introduction of your college essay.

If the purpose of the introduction is to *hook* the reader, to pull the reader in with something perhaps unexpected—to urge the reader to continue reading—then we can think of the conclusion as a *hint* at that opening—as a way to sort of respond to how the reader reacted when they read that unexpected opening, when they shook their head and said, "What the—?"

In the last session, I re-shared the introductory sentence of Lucy's *Stay-Upper* Essay:

> *My name is Lucy, and deep down, I'm what I've been since I was six years old. I'm a stay upper.*

In her essay, the author explains that the term *stay upper* was given to children when they reached six. The *stay uppers* didn't have to nap anymore and were allowed to stay at the school for an extended day program when all the four- and five-year-old kids went home.

The main message of that essay focused on an immersive adventure experience that extended the notion of what it meant for that essayist to be a stay upper, i.e., to be a full participant in every facet of life, from the ordinary to the extraordinary.

The stay upper's conclusion?

> *Despite whatever new challenges, experiences, and friends await, I will approach them with the same excitement, energy, curiosity, and love that I felt that day I turned six years old and became a stay upper.*

Cole's *Tapping-In* essay, which I share in the addendum, starts with this opening:

> *The sound of my dad's guitar was the soundtrack to my life as I learned to crawl, walk, and speak, and when I was nine I picked up a guitar and never looked back. The next years were filled with endless practice, frustration, and general wonderment at how my father manipulated the strings so easily.*

Shortly after this introduction, the essayist writes about an occasion in which he is playing guitar with his father on stage and finally musters the courage to tap his father on the shoulder to let him know he's finally ready to play a guitar solo. The essay concludes with these two sentences:

> *Though I have so many interests outside of the music arena, this medium continues to be a deeply satisfying creative outlet. But even more than that, it has become a symbol for me of the world that opened up when I tapped on my father's shoulder and asked him to step aside.*

It's important to keep in mind that there is no such thing as *the* perfect opening or the perfect conclusion to a college essay. There are as many ways to start an essay as there are to conclude it.

REVISITING THE PERSONAL ESSAY CHECKLIST

Way back in one of our earlier sessions I said that some of the best College Application Personal Essays share the characteristics of great personal essays. This is a great time to sit down with your C.A.P.E. at your side and check the items on the list that align with your essay. If necessary, look back on page 37 to see the more detailed descriptions of the characteristics.

A reminder

It isn't critical that *all* personal essays have *all* of these characteristics—and as we've noted earlier, you can't mad-lib your way through this essay, but the vast majority of these elements really are present in good personal essays.

Read through your **C**ollege **A**pplication **P**ersonal **E**ssay to determine if it can be said to contain the following characteristics:

- ☐ My C.A.P.E. has an *apparent* subject and a *deeper* subject
- ☐ My C.A.P.E. is not afraid of intimacy (close authorial presence and distance)
- ☐ My C.A.P.E. is artful, literary, and well crafted
- ☐ The voice and tone of my C.A.P.E. is conversational
- ☐ My C.A.P.E. isn't afraid to be emotional
- ☐ My C.A.P.E. shares a range of emotions
- ☐ My C.A.P.E. yearns to reveal the truth
- ☐ My C.A.P.E. is not afraid to examine my limitations and inconsistencies
- ☐ The narrator of my C.A.P.E. is reliable
- ☐ My C.A.P.E. explores what it doesn't know
- ☐ My C.A.P.E. isn't afraid to examine the small things in life
- ☐ My C.A.P.E. is not afraid of humor
- ☐ My C.A.P.E. isn't out to be loved by the reader
- ☐ My C.A.P.E. thinks against itself, challenges its own conventional thought
- ☐ My C.A.P.E. is flexible in form and style; it's digressive, associative
- ☐ My C.A.P.E. tells a good story
- ☐ My C.A.P.E. is elaborate, explanatory, and thorough
- ☐ My C.A.P.E. is uniquely singular (individual) as well as universal

SOME OTHER THINGS TO THINK ABOUT IN THE WORLD OF REVISION...

It's always nice if you happen to have people in your world who are great writers. It's even nicer if they know you well and they like you. And it's a total bonus if they have some sense of how important the College Application Personal Essay is.

If they do have some sense of its importance, they're more likely to take the time to help you through the revision process.

But in any case, this section will provide you with a few more helpful bits of advice.

Word Count, Finally...

I've been telling you on and off for more than a hundred pages to not think about word count, but it's time to start thinking about it.

CTI: Cut the Inessential

One of the things I've always included in my comments on English essays is the initialism CTI, which stands for Cut the Inessential.

Sometimes I'll add a few words in parentheses, something to the tune of "rewrite this sentence with fifteen fewer words," or "knock off one hundred words from this page for five extra points."

When faced with this suggestion, students never eliminate essential language. They eliminate unnecessary words here and there, and sometimes they knock off entire sentences or paragraphs.

If you have taken my suggestion to *just write* without regard for editing, then you're going to find a lot of inessential language in your first few drafts.

Take a look at your current draft—let's say it clocks in at 1857 words. Go through it and tell yourself you're going to read it through a few times, and you're going to knock off one hundred words each time through.

You probably won't have too much trouble doing this the first few times. It will get trickier the closer you come to the 650-word limit.

When it starts getting tricky, it may be time to get another set of eyes on the essay.

Let Your Essay Sit between Drafts

My suggestion to set your essay aside before the revision fits here as well. In between each of your drafts, it's not a bad idea to let the essay sit. Coming back to each of these revisions after a break is a bit like coming back to it with a fresh perspective.

Another Set of Eyes

When it gets tough to edit your essay down any further, it might be a good time to ask someone else on Team You to take a look at your essay for the purpose of bringing it closer to the 650-word limit.

It may be helpful if this new set of eyes belongs to someone you've already worked with on your essay. What you want to be careful about, though, is having *too* many people look at your essay. The more people you show it to, the more likely you are to get mixed messages about the content. It's best to limit it to the one or two or few people who know you well and are good writers and editors. (At this point in your life, you probably have at least a short list of people you shouldn't show your work to.)

When you show the essay to someone, make sure you tell them what you're asking of them. Definitely tell them that you need to knock off three hundred words—or whatever the case may be—but also feel free to tell them that you're interested in their thoughts about the essay so far. You can give them this list of questions you've already asked yourself.

- If an admissions officer reads this discovery draft just as it is, how might they think of me as a student on their campus?
- Would they have a sense of my personality?
- Would they see me as a student who could thrive on their college campus?
- Would they be excited about what I might add to their school?
- Does the essay suggest how I might interact with others?
- Does the essay distinguish me from the rest of the applicant pool?
- What are other aspects of your personality that this essay does not address?

Title?

Someone once told me that the three most direct lines of communication the reader has with the written work are the title, the introduction, and the conclusion. We've previously touched on the importance of the introduction and the conclusion, but I haven't said anything about the title thus far. The simple truth is that your essay doesn't need a title. Hopefully, it's a clear enough essay that its readers will sort of create a title for it. That's how the *stay-upper* essay and the *tapping-in* essay received their titles.

If your essay turns out to be an essay that goes viral out there in the world, it will certainly pick up a title on its journey to viral. But it doesn't need one, and in my estimation, it probably shouldn't have one. It's a little bit like trying to give yourself a nickname. Leave it up to the people around you to do that.

Introduction

I spent some time talking about the access intro in a previous chapter. Well, now is a good time to return to it. Take another look at these elements of a good introduction and see if you're still happy with your opening line.

- Is it an attention-getter?
- Is it memorable?
- Does it pull the reader into the story?
- Does it do more than one thing?

Conclusion

Now, take another look at the conclusion. Consider these questions as you read it again.

- Does it seem like a proper conclusion for the essay?
- Is it memorable?
- Does it tie the essay together?
- Does it hint at the opening?

Don't Rely on Computer Spelling and Grammar Check

Look, you've made it through three years of high school. You already know this. The spell check and grammar check features on your laptop are not bad places to *start* your revision process, but no computer is going to be better at revision than a human being with a discerning eye.

The Best Advice on Learning How to Revise: Become an Editor for Your Peers

There are some people who just love quotes. I know a guy who quotes other people so much that I'm not sure he'd have anything to say if it weren't for the statements of other people. My own father used to watch this ridiculous TV channel that played nothing but quotes and terrible music. He could watch it all day.

I'm not that crazy about quotes, but there's a fiction writer named Steve Almond who wrote a sentence about the value of peer editing that's so much what I believe that I'm actually angry with him for this quote. I don't know him, but I feel like we're fighting now. I should have been the one to write it.

> *"To look at the work of your peers, and learn how to explain with kindness and precision, the nature of their mistakes is, in fact, how you learn to diagnose your own work."*

> *Steve Almond*

I founded a great little magazine called *Polyphony Lit* in 2005, and it has evolved entirely around the principle of peer editing. That magazine has convinced me that there is no better way to become a great writer than by looking at the work of other writers and learning how to language—precisely, generously, and kindly—how their writing works, how it *behaves* and how it *misbehaves*, how it fails and how it succeeds.

One of the great certainties of the college application process is that you're going through the experience with your peers. Yes, I know you're busy with your own application, but trust me when I say that every opportunity you have to language why something works or doesn't work with anyone's writing is another opportunity to improve your own writing.

Some Advice for Peer Editing

1) Take every opportunity you can to read and edit your peers' College Application Personal Essays.
2) If you find something that works beautifully in an essay, try to find the perfect language to articulate what it is and why it works.
3) If you find something that doesn't quite work, try to find the perfect language to articulate why it doesn't.

HOW TO KNOW WHEN YOU'RE FINALLY THERE

I have stories that I've revised more than sixty times. Some of those stories are published in books, and when I read from them at various events, I still make changes here and there.

When I coach students through their C.A.P.E., I tell them they're done when they can set their C.A.P.E. aside for the night, reread it in the morning, and be able to say the following things about it:

1) I'm happy with this essay as it is.
2) This essay is the result of meaningful self-reflection.
3) This essay is true.
4) This essay reveals important elements of who I am.
5) This essay is 650 or fewer words.

Addendum

Sample Prompts

In this section we'll share the original responses that Lucy, one of our recent C.A.P.E. course participants, wrote to several of the C.A.P.E. course prompts, and we'll follow this with her expanded responses to the same prompts. I think they provide good examples of the thoroughness and thoughtfulness that I hope you'll use in your approach to expanding your prompts.

Our participant selected from among her prompt responses what she felt revealed her true character most.

Please note: A simple word count on our participant's expanded responses reveals that this material clocks in at just under 2800 words. I note this to show that Lucy did not allow the word count to restrict her as she began this process.

I've organized the material by leading with the original prompt and then supplying her expanded responses.

My hope is that the example provides you with some ideas as to how to take the prompt responses that you've expanded and explored and use them to begin putting shape to your C.A.P.E.

SAMPLES OF LUCY'S ORIGINAL AND EXPANDED RESPONSES

Prompt: A teacher who has had a positive impact on you.

Original Prompt Response: Mrs. C., my seventh-grade teacher.

Expanded Response: Mrs. C. was the first female teacher I really valued and appreciated. And don't get me wrong, I have had many strong female role models in my life (my mom, sisters, grandmas, and aunts) but she was the first woman outside of my family that I was truly awed by. She would go throughout the day on her own terms no matter how the stupid seventh-grade boys would treat her. She was hilarious and didn't care how many people laughed at her jokes, she was also so strong and she was one of my best support systems. She always taught me how to deal with my peers (in a civil way) who discounted my voice or didn't respect me, as well as teaching me how to be an all-around confident woman. I will always be grateful for the lessons she taught me. I don't think she really knows how much her constant support and belief in me mattered to me.

Some boys in class were disrespectful and discounted her words. I just remember she wouldn't care what others really thought of her and if people didn't agree with what she had to say or how she wanted to do something she didn't let it affect her. It was as though she could walk on water if she put her mind to it. I think that all the girls really respected her because we all wanted to be just like her. I'm not sure if the boys felt this way, though. I think of her a lot if I am in a situation where I feel as though my voice is being drowned out because I am a young woman, or when people don't trust my opinion in a certain situation. And because I know she wouldn't be happy with me if I gave up on anything, I don't. Also, it can be really hard to be a girl in high school, but she truly taught me to value myself and what I personally bring to the table and I will always be grateful for that.

Prompt: Early memory

Original Prompt Response: Sitting in the garden with my grandmother and mom

Expanded Response: We went to the botanic gardens and we sat on a field of grass and we ate tiny marshmallows and drank hot chocolate. I remember running around the grounds and through the fields and just feeling so happy. I remember how happy my grandma and mom were and I loved seeing that more than anything. It means a lot because I am so close with them now, and I feel like this was the first time I really bonded with them. Also it's where I think my love for nature really came from.

Prompt: Early memory

Original Prompt Response: being a stay-upper

Expanded Response: Being a stay-upper is when you are the oldest in your class during ages three to six and you get to "stay up" the whole day while the people younger than you napped or went home. I remember sitting in the different sections of the classroom and eating cookies and drinking tea and feeling so cool because I was staying up.

Prompt: Favorite photo

Original Prompt Response: the photo of me and my family in the trees at Weller Lake/American Lake

Expanded Response: We are in this little canopy of trees right on American lake eating my favorite meal of all time (cheese, bread, crackers, and salami we eat at every hike), after we had just finished a three-hour hike. I'm about five years old and I will never forget that day and that picture because it is when hikes in aspen with my family became my favorite thing to do.

Prompt: If you did not have this formative experience, you might be a totally different person.

Original Prompt Response: my middle school experience

Expanded Response: I went to a very tiny Montessori middle school and I had a very different experience than many of my high school friends. I learned how to add from blocks on a rug, and I learned how to write by tracing cursive cutouts. Also, in seventh grade when my friends [from my new school] were going to parties and socializing, I was watching Harry Potter on Saturday nights and having a blast! I feel as though Near North was its own little island that made me a different person than all of my friends. I was in a bubble because all I knew was my school and the values it taught me, nothing else mattered. That is until I got to high school and realized how different my middle school experience was.

This experience made me different from my peers in not only high school, but I think throughout my life and I am incredibly grateful for it. I used to be sad about it and feel left out, but now I appreciate the values it taught me and how it has shaped me. Knowing I would always think about things a little bit differently from other people has really shaped my high school experience. It made me know that if I was doing things a little bit differently from my friends, that was okay because I was raised in such a different environment and just because it's different doesn't mean that it is wrong. Also, having a Montessori education has shaped the ways in which I approach different situations as well as problem-solve. I think that my [new school] friends missed out on having an untraditional learning experience that taught me how to be creative with my learning and think outside the box.

Prompt: Describe a positive educational experience.

Original Prompt Response: Any experiment in chemistry or when Dr. H had that talk with us.

Expanded Response: Sophomore year I took chemistry and it was the first time I really knew science was going to be my thing. We would do experiments like changing the color of fire or changing the density of a substance, and I couldn't stop smiling the whole time (this and my obvious Harry Potter obsession is what proved to my friends that I really am a nerd...). I would look forward to class every day while my friends dreaded it, and the tests became a little too easy for me because of how interested I was in the topics.

The source of my love for science is a mystery. I don't know where it came from or why it's so strong, but the thought of any sort of experiment makes me ridiculously happy.

It might come from the fact that I went to a Montessori school. But I am also a naturally curious person and a lot of science has to do with figuring out how things work and why. How to solve problems. I love figuring out why exactly things in our bodies or environment do the things that they do and how. It is utterly amazing to me how something in life urges you to ask a question, and you can perform an experiment and find your answer.

I love knowing exactly how things work, and science gives me an opportunity to figure out everything I want to figure out. I also loved how different my reaction (toward science?) was from the other kids in the class because it made my interest feel singular and unique.

I loved seeing how unexpected things could combine and react to explain something I had been witnessing my whole life. So often, the answers seem utterly simple, but simultaneously so complex.

Freshman year is when I took Dr. H's class. I was in a class with a lot of great and intelligent girls, but also some obnoxious boys. In one class, we had a huge discussion about some current events. These current events were pretty sensitive topics for certain people and they were very controversial. It pretty much turned into a debate between me and another girl against three guys. I was extremely knowledgeable about this topic and had great points, but the guys would just laugh at my words and discount all of my information. Dr. H sat by and watched this happen for the rest of the class until it ended. She then asked all of the boys to leave the room but asked the girls to stay. She told us that as intelligent women who will be in the workforce, we would have to deal with people like that in our futures and we better start learning how to deal with it. And I definitely learned some very valuable tactics and lessons from that class.

I don't remember exactly what the conversation was or the things the boys said; I just remember I would prepare a very strong and well-presented point that I was excited for and all they would do was laugh and make fun of me. I remember feeling extremely pushed aside and not important. I hated feeling so easily put down and embarrassed. I felt so weak and I hated most of all that I was letting them get to me.

Prompt: Describe a time you felt very different from others.

Original Prompt Response: Iceland trip

Expanded Response: I went to Iceland this summer with eleven strangers and had the most magical time of my life. I was completely detached from the real world and from all of my responsibilities. It was just two weeks full of pushing myself and my body to new limits and it felt amazing. I felt like an instrumental part of the world, worthy of attention in a place of belonging with nature, connection. It was a total immersion experience, an escape from covid and college stuff, friend groups. We backpacked six days, kayaked for four days. I was truly able to be myself and I was surrounded constantly by nature and by people who really valued my presence. It was an incredibly perfect experience and I met just amazing people. I was also doing what I love most, hiking, camping, and doing fun activities. I didn't have to think about anything else, and my whole world was just this little beautiful country and nothing else mattered.

It never got dark. Land of fire and ice. Tectonic plates, insane natural spectacular things, hot springs.

It was a camping trip as well as a cultural trip. We back-country hiked for a week and we also kayaked and spent time in the city. I was in nature for so long and had nothing to do but cook, hike, and set up camp. I just really felt like I belonged and my friends constantly wanted me around. I felt like I was always adding something to the experience and people really valued and liked what I had to say. I was shown this when I had to miss out on one hike and everyone on the trip couldn't have been happier to see me when I returned and wouldn't stop talking about how different it was without me. This could be because I felt so at home in the nature and I could completely be myself. They definitely saw the world through a lens that I personally use and that was great also and it helped me connect with them. It taught me how much I value simple pleasure in life and the kind of people that I like to be surrounded by. It taught me how much I love being able to be the positive one of the group that helped everyone get through the hard days. It also showed me that no matter how scared I am for unknown adventures, I should always push myself to do them because I'll never know the happiness they could give me.

Then I was ripped out of my oasis and plopped right back into the real world without any transition. It was scary. I hadn't been on a phone at all and texting my friends and family who I hadn't talked to in so long felt like a burden and overwhelming. It felt like all they talked about was nothing but small talk, reality shows. I wanted to be back in Iceland talking about things that had nothing to do with phones.

I hated it. Why wasn't I excited to tell my parents all about my incredible time? Why was I questioning all of my relationships at home just because I had made such strong ones in Iceland? I loved my life at home, but getting this taste of traveling throughout a country with no responsibilities or expectations just felt so freeing and I knew I was going to miss it so much. It was hard to connect again with my people at home because they didn't understand the experience that I had and it was so hard to explain exactly what it was like. I also think it was harder to connect with certain people who don't share my love for adventure and hiking more than normal. I felt like my trip changed me and people didn't really understand that. I reached a kind of rare happiness and I was scared I would never reach it again.

This is the only way I think I can explain it. Have you ever had a moment where life kind of pauses for a second and everything around you freezes and it is just you and your surroundings that matter? And you just sit there and think wow. Life is pretty freaking amazing right now and I am so beyond happy. That was the whole trip for me.

Prompt: When is a time you were filled with hope?

Original Prompt Response: When the world started healing from Covid-19.

Expanded Response: This was a really important time for me because when I started to be able to do normal things again, I appreciated them so much more. Even the little things, like passing people in the hallway at school. That interaction sparks so much more joy for me now because I know how it feels to live without it. This is the same for a lot of human interaction.

Prompt: A list of at least ten things you have, tangible or otherwise, that speak to who you are.

Original Prompt Response: My interest in bio and how the world works.

Expanded Response: My interest in biology and ecology started with these nature shows that my dad and I would watch every Sunday night. They would follow certain animals and organisms around during their lives and explain what they were doing and why. I was always so interested in these little creatures and I loved seeing all of the amazing things that they did. It was so incredible to me that our world's little parts functioned in such closeness to one another and each part depended on another. I knew from these shows, and my interest that stemmed from them, my job would have something to do with biology and the natural world.

Prompt: A character trait of people that drives you crazy.

Original Prompt Response: When people are negative and downers.

Expanded Response: I cannot stand when people go out of their way to point out the negative sides of situations and when they don't try to make things better. I think that's because I always try to make the best of situations so when they don't happen, I don't get mad. Like when I am playing a field hockey game and we are losing, or it's cold or it's rainy, and all people do is just complain about everything and not try to make the situation fun.

Or when I am doing any sort of physical activity (running, hiking, climbing) and the people who I am with are complaining and not trying to make the most out of the situation.

Sample Outline: Tapping In Essay

I. Hook: an interesting story to pull the reader in immediately. It might be funny, surprising, unexpected, powerful, even ridiculous.

Through my childhood, the sound of my dad's guitar was the soundtrack to my life as I learned to crawl, walk, and speak, and when I was nine I picked up a guitar and never looked back. The next years were filled with endless practice, frustration, and a general wonderment at how my father manipulated the strings so easily.

II. Brief history of essayist playing in a band with his father.

III. Essayist introduces his growing interest but lack of confidence in taking over his father's role as the guitar soloist on stage. He finally taps on his father's shoulder to take over the solo.

IV. Body of the essay: essayist extends the idea of "tapping in" to suggest a more complete participation in social, academic, and extracurricular arenas.

V. Closer: A brief return to the moment on stage when the essayist tapped on his father's shoulder to take on the guitar solo.

Tapping In Essay

Through my childhood, the sound of my dad's guitar was the soundtrack to my life as I learned to crawl, walk, and speak, and when I was nine I picked up a guitar and never looked back. The next years were filled with endless practice, frustration, and a general wonderment at how my father manipulated the strings so easily.

Years later, in high school, my father and I were asked to accompany the school orchestra on Aerosmith's "Walk This Way." Much of that night is a blur, but I do remember my father's blazing guitar solo and the standing ovation that followed. It had a lasting effect on me.

Eventually, I started playing with my father's band, and for one show, I rehearsed the solo of the Stones' "Sympathy for the Devil" until I knew it by heart. But I lacked the confidence to play it live. Every time my father asked me if I wanted to play it, I said, "No." But one night, the drums kicked in and the audience started to dance and the solo came around, and something shifted. My father played the first bar of the solo, and for some strange reason I just felt ready. I tapped him on the shoulder, and he stepped aside.

And I played.

Musicians describe out-of-body experiences and this was one of those moments for me. Every worry I had fell away and my fingers took over. And when it ended, the audience erupted in a fury of applause.

That solo was less than two minutes, but the idea of tapping shoulders and heading into new, vulnerable experiences has become the new soundtrack to my life.

When my three best friends moved the summer after that solo, I felt stranded and lost. I was a shy kid, and the idea of branching out was scary. For a long time I was paralyzed by the idea of talking to new kids. But something akin to that shift on the stage happened in my life, then, and I realized that the only way I would be happy was if I branched out. That branching out was the best decision I've ever made. That branching out helped me to see, in my relationships with others, what I had to offer. It helped me to become the version of myself I've always wanted to be.

It was that same metaphorical "tapping in" that allowed me to pursue an interest I've had since childhood. In my sophomore year I signed up for an entrepreneurship class filled primarily with juniors and seniors—entirely unfamiliar and frightening faces. Worse, a major component of the class was a terrifying presentation in front of the class. But I stuck with it, and an experience I thought might be tragic turned out to be a great strength. The final project became an award-winning success when my group won first runner-up in a multi-state entrepreneurship competition.

What I came to realize, though, is that every success—for me, at least—only becomes another opportunity to take on a bigger, often more terrifying challenge.

That competition, for example, led to my being offered an internship at an auto auction company. While I was excited about it, I also knew I would be the youngest employee in the company. And, of course, all those ancient insecurities surfaced. But once I took the train to the city and walked into the offices, I surprised myself again, tapped out the old version of me, and soon earned a spot as a valuable member of a team that has contributed in major ways to several projects.

I have many interests outside of the music arena, but this medium continues to be a deeply satisfying outlet. But even more than that, it had become a symbol for me of the world that opened up when I tapped on my father's shoulder and asked him to step aside.

Sample Outline: Stay-Upper Essay

I. Hook: an interesting story to pull the reader in immediately. It might be funny, surprising, unexpected, powerful, even ridiculous.

For two long years at my school, I had to contend with measly half-days of school and stupid mandatory naps, but at six years old, I became a stay upper.

II. Brief explanation of what it means to be a *stay upper*.

III. Extend the idea of what it means to be a stay-upper, to be a full participant in all of life, from the ordinary to the extraordinary moments.

IV. Body of the essay: A recent experience that represents the full embodiment of what it means to be a stay upper.

V. Closer: some kind of return, however brief, to the stay-upper hook.

Despite whatever new challenges, experiences, and friends await, I will approach them with the same excitement, energy, curiosity, and love that I felt that day I turned six years old and became a stay upper.

Stay-Upper Essay

For two long years at my school, I had to contend with measly half-days of school and stupid mandatory naps, but at six years old, I became a stay upper. All day I could participate in the wonders of learning and exploring—I could learn to count by stacking blocks, and how to write by tracing cursive cutouts. It was a new world!

That stay-upper spirit stayed with me through middle school where I fell in love with science and the world of experiments.

It wasn't until I got to high school that I realized how different I was. My excitement for learning and exploring and deep human connection distinguished me from so many others. And in the midst of trying to navigate social pressures, I felt myself slip into a kind of half-participation in life.

The drama and the realities of life came to a head during my junior year. I needed to get away—or maybe not so much to get away as to find my way back. So, I signed up for a rigorous and challenging trip.

In less than a few short weeks I stood at the base of a mountain with eleven strangers and a fifty-pound backpack, in a country where the sun never set.

The trip began with a treacherous day of mountain climbing through a storm of wind and snow—day one and already our muscles ached, but I felt an instant comfort among these strangers. As we rested and thawed in our tents, played cards, and discussed the day's terrific and brutal type-two fun, I felt myself returning. Despite my knotted hair and the remnant pain, I was happy.

As the days unfolded, the rigors of the trip grew, and the weight of our backpacks seemed to grow as well. The boys in my group, who called themselves warriors, pleaded for frequent breaks.

So I lugged my thousand-pound backpack onto my aching shoulders and urged them forward by helping them visualize our return to camp. And we kept moving.

I felt a power in harnessing my voice as a leader in inspiring them, in renewing their spirit.

I challenged them, I cajoled them out of their tents to explore the mysteries of that world—the beauty of geothermal springs and brilliant pink flowers juxtaposed against black sand. We found joy in challenges.

I felt my peers valued what I had to say and what I brought to the group. I was adding something to their experience. I felt this especially when I had to miss out on one hike, and everyone seemed so happy to see me when I returned. It taught me how much I value simple pleasures in life. It reminded me of the kind of people that I want to be surrounded by. It reminded me that only by pushing myself toward new adventures would I understand the happiness they gave me.

In my tent on the last night of the trip I sat by myself to take it all in. Everything around me seemed so still. It was just me and my surroundings. Wow! I thought. Life is pretty freaking amazing. I was beyond happy, and I wanted to never let it go.

But a part of me was reluctant to return to the real world. What if I had achieved a rare happiness that I would never reach again?

The experience had taught me, though, that I was in control. I had returned to myself. And if I could remain true to myself, then this was a happiness I could reach again.

I'm not sure what the future holds for me, but I have promised myself that I will stay true. Despite whatever new challenges, experiences, and friends await, I will approach them with the same excitement, energy, curiosity, and love that I felt that day I turned six years old and became a stay upper.

Final Thoughts Before Leaving...

Way back in the earliest pages of *The C.A.P.E. Crusade*, I wrote something that is well worth repeating. Whatever your scores and statistics, your GPA, your SATs, ACTs, and RBIs, "you are *more* than those numbers."

And, it is a truth worth expanding on as well. You're also more than your College Application Personal Essay.

Whether your essay is part of a successful application to two colleges or to twenty-two colleges, know that you are far more than the 650 words that comprise your C.A.P.E. You're more than all the stories you've been a part of, more than the service hours, more than the points scored, more than the extracurriculars, more than the friends you've lost and found, more than every book you've ever read, more than all the occasions and experiences you can recall, and more than the thousands of important and ordinary days that are too foggy, too tricky, too elusive—too *something*—to remember. You're more than the colleges you get into, more than the colleges you don't get into, more than the thousands of colleges you didn't apply to, and more than the colleges you still don't know about.

You're all of these things and more, and you're on your way to growing and unfolding in unimaginable ways.

AND A BIT OF ADVICE AS YOU MOVE ON...

1) Enjoy your senior year.
2) There is a very fine line between counting down the days and wishing time away. Fight the temptation.

3) Be kind to underclassmen and women; you will be one again soon.
4) Live as though younger students are watching you in order to figure out how to be seniors.

And thank you for letting me be part of this crusade of yours.

—Billy Lombardo

Acknowledgments

A gigantic thank you to Franko Tempone and Jimmy Joyce, my great old friends and former colleagues, for their friendship, advice, companionship, and support over many years. Thanks to the scores of students I've worked with at dozens of schools around the world, from Chicago to Shanghai, but especially to Lucy Norris, Kate Guynn, Owen Garland, and Cole Jiaras, who have given me their blessing to use their work here. Thanks also to Gina Frangello (whom I'll be thanking forever) and to Emily Rapp Black, who, along with Gina, inspired me to do the work that resulted in *The C.A.P.E. Crusade.* Thanks also to Mary O'Malley, Rhody Davis, Anne Frame Sheppard, and Sara Connell, and especially to my person, Amy Danzer.

About the Author

Billy Lombardo is the author of poetry, fiction, essays, plays, reviews, interviews, articles, screenplays, and more. His books include *The Logic of a Rose: Chicago Stories, The Man with Two Arms, Morning Will Come, How to Hold a Woman,* and *Meanwhile, Roxy Mourns.* He is a Nelson Algren Award winner and the founder of *Polyphony Lit,* a student-run, international literary magazine for high school writers and editors. He is the founder of The Writing Pros/e, a writing and editing business. He teaches English at Trinity High School for Girls in River Forest, Illinois. He is a marathoner, a bestselling ghostwriter, and works one-on-one with a limited number of clients. He lives in Chicago with Amy and Valentino.